IDENTIFYING

WITH

THE INFINITE

OTHER BOOKS IN THIS SERIES

Coming Into Freedom:
H. Emily Cady's Lessons in Truth for the 21st Century

Experiencing the Miracle:
The Essence of the Course in Miracles for the 21st Century

Unveiling Your Hidden Power:
Emma Curtis Hopkins' Metaphysics for the 21st Century

Each of these volumes is Ruth L. Miller's modern-language version of the original text. She has removed gender bias, used shorter sentences and paragraphs, cited sacred sources from multiple spiritual traditions, and has added summary points, headings, and exercises for each section.

AN OVERVIEW OF THEIR TEACHINGS

Healing by Words Alone
Understanding America's New Thought Healers & Teachers
By Ruth L. Miller

Identifying

With

The Infinite

LILLIAN DEWATERS' SCIENCE OF
ASCENSION FOR THE 21ST CENTURY

modern interpretation by
Ruth L. Miller

SPIRIT BOOKS

Portal
Center
Press

www.portalcenterpress.com

Identifying with the Infinite: Lillian DeWaters' Science of
Ascension for the 21st Century
© 2024 by Ruth L. Miller

Published by **SPIRIT BOOKS,**
an imprint of Portal Center Press
www.portalcenterpress.com

ISBN: 978-1-936902-52-1

Printed in the U.S.A.

DEDICATION

To those who are ready to know and practice
their true Identity

CONTENTS

EDITOR'S NOTE

A marvelous little book with a bright red cover came to me when an elderly minister retired and shared her library with those around her. Among the many lovely resources in the box, this one seemed to glow, insisting that I take it home. As I picked it up, I saw the title: *The Science of Ascension, A Study of the Absolute.* The author's name was unfamiliar to me. It was a 1960 edition of a book that had been published in 1929.

For the first few weeks, in my sometimes overwhelmingly busy schedule, it seemed that all I could do was dip into its pages to sample what was there. After a few such samplings, though, it became clear that it wanted a thorough study. So I arranged for a group to study it with me.

Our first session, however, made it clear that the writing style — as with so many of the teachers who grew up in the 19th century — was putting my fellow students off, and they were not getting "the meat" of what was being offered.

So, once again, as I have with almost a dozen other works,[1] I found myself going through the text page by page, typing the material in shorter sentences, with less gender bias, and adding references to spiritual traditions other than Christianity that offer similar teachings. Then, as always, I reviewed again and again what

---

[1] Simon & Schuster's Library of Hidden Knowledge include my modernized interpretations of works by Emerson, Drummond, Haanel, Shinn, Allen, Wattles, and Hopkins, to which Portal Center Press has added Troward and this title. WiseWoman Press has published my interpretations of works by Emilie Cady and Emma Curtis Hopkins.

I had typed, cleaning it up still further, making it as clear and concise as modern readers demand. I then concluded each chapter with summary points and questions to ponder.

Why did I take this time and effort? I certainly don't need to put yet another book on the publisher's shelves! No, it was because the material, itself, demanded being made available to modern students of applied metaphysics — or, as Emma Curtis Hopkins put it, "applied mysticism."

As I explored the pages of DeWaters' book, I realized that she, too, was a Hopkins student, and that this was her expansion on Hopkins' twelfth lesson, where students are encouraged to realize their identity as transcendent beings with transcendent powers.

DeWaters had clearly experienced the reality of that lesson and had seen the potential for all humanity to achieve a state of consciousness that far exceeds the norm in our Western, colonialized culture. She could see, hear, feel, and know that we are not "cogs in a machine," nor simply consumers of things and ideas, nor even citizens of nations, but the very embodiment of the infinite Creative Spirit, with all the qualities that we call divine. And she found a way to help others do the same.

In this text, then, what she created is not so much a book to be read as a set of lessons to work through. Each chapter, therefore, has points to ponder and practices to explore. If you do one chapter a week, reading it through and then contemplating the summary points and the exercises, using a journal to track your responses, you'll get far more out of it than if you simply read it.

As you work through these pages may you, too, come to know — and realize (make real in your experience) — your true Identity.

~rlm
Florence, Oregon

FROM DEWATERS' PREFACE

Humanity's understandings of the nature of the Universe, of what we call God, and of the Self of each person, are becoming clearer and more complete with every generation. This is happening as humanity's thoughts are gently rising from a materialist view to a truer understanding of what we are and what being is. Every new stage in our lives and in our world offers us a clearer and more practical experience of what a perfect life might be.

In the process, more and more people are beginning to become aware of an Absolute Science, one that transcends material laws and reveals our true identity. This Absolute Science shows us that, as we become aware of our true being as Spirit, we are no longer bound by the beliefs and misunderstandings of the material world, but are rising to the limitless state of being that is our true nature. It demonstrates that the universe is perfect and that we may experience perfect being *in* this universe, and use our true power to create, manifest, and maintain perfect joy, peace, and love, always.

Historically, this science has been like "a lamp shining in the darkness." People have been attached to material beliefs and experience, often called "the darkness." As a result, the books, teachers, and instructions that have presented what they call "the kingdom of heaven," or *Atman,* as being within us and at hand have been like lamps lighting the way out of that darkness. For everyone who has been able to grasp the message: "the darkness doesn't apprehend it," they've shown a higher and deeper experience of the ever-present Spirit of Life.

For those who, having encountered that light, choose to learn this Science and ascend from the material world to a higher way of being, the way is filled with blessings. It must be so, for how could anyone achieve a more complete understanding of life without a richer and fuller experience of their own joyful being? After all, as the ancient scriptures tell us "What you see, that you are," which is to say: what we focus our attention on is what we become.

There are some people who are slow to accept the advanced ideas presented by this Science, and so they come to a standstill in their understanding—and in their demonstration of the many forms of good in their lives. Since it's the nature of the universe to expand, our consciousness, being an aspect of our universe, must continue to expand to continue to be in harmony with its own true nature. This means we must (that is, can't not) continue to advance in our understanding of Spirit. We *must* (can't not) come to realize Spirit as the essence of all that is, and continue to grow in our demonstration of its continually expanding perfection as the only Reality. It's *not possible* to remain in darkness! We *must* (can't not) ultimately accept and prove to ourselves that all existence is, in fact, Spirit in expression.

More, as we choose to live by this spiritual Truth, we begin to experience a deeper understanding of ourselves as spiritual beings. We become aware of and realize (which is to say, make real to our experience) our true perfection—our oneness with the Source, Power, and Presence of all that is, what we call Spirit, here, now, always.

Learning the power of Spirit over the senses, and choosing Science over our old beliefs, our demonstration of what we know to be good in our lives becomes easy and natural, and we feel reborn into a life of deep joy, peace, and harmony. As our senses are uplifted from focusing on the material world with its limitations, we begin to perceive, retain, and practice the Reality of our being, and we no longer make things happen that are disharmonious with our true nature. We experience the fulfillment of the promise: "If you abide in me (the divine state of consciousness) and my word (divine understanding, mental framework) abides in you, you shall ask whatever you choose, and it shall be done."

This realization of our oneness with Spirit is the state of being that the ancients called the Christ. It is "the mind that was in Christ Jesus," as taught in the Christian New Testament, and also was in Krishna, as taught in the Hindu *Bhagavad Gita*. And, as both of those teachers told their followers, each of us must ultimately attain this state of being—it is who and what we truly are, behind all the thoughts and beliefs we have taken on in our human journey. *All of us* will experience all the glories of the One, All-encompassing Spirit when we accept our own true Selfhood.

The possibility of such an experience raises the question: why would anyone give power to physical experiences, psychological principles, or material processes, if such things block or hinder our experience of total freedom and power in such a glorious Reality? The answer is found in our old sense-based beliefs. They are "the darkness which does not apprehend the light."

When we choose the state of being that is our potential, when we follow the light, we make rapid progress in overcoming all false beliefs. We finally let go of any beliefs based in ideas that sin, sickness, bondage, and poverty are real and must be overcome that we previously accepted.

The time has now come for all humanity, and especially those who have picked up this book, to demonstrate to our own satisfaction, and to the world around us, this understanding, this knowing, and this way of being. For centuries, now, seekers of spiritual understanding have been bringing the teachings of the One Mind, as expressed by Jesus, Krishna, Lao Tse[2], and others, more and more clearly into common understanding. So, now that the truth of those teachings has been made clear, it's time for us to understand and practice them.

∞

---

[2] LaoTse means "ancient master" and is the official author of the Taoist text, *The Tao te Ching*.

PART ONE

DEWATERS' LESSONS
INTERPRETED

CHAPTER ONE

DELIVERANCE WITHOUT EFFORT

In the Christian New Testament, Jesus the Nazarene is described as having practiced and taught a Science that not only enabled him to help and bless others on their plane of existence, but lifted him up into a reality of consciousness that we call *ascension*. This Jesus then prophesized that a new vision would come to those who follow his teachings, a vision that is greater than healing the sick, even greater than raising the dead.

Isn't seeing an end to sickness greater than healing, and isn't being immune to death greater than raising the dead? That's what's offered by this new vision, this state of consciousness. It's a state of consciousness in which we don't just overcome undesirable conditions, *those conditions no longer exist*.

In such a state of consciousness, even the *idea* that anyone need overcome an undesirable condition no longer exists. One begins to experience a new kind of heaven and earth, and to see one's own immortality and transcending glory.[3]

RISING UP

If someone says that their body is sick, their wallet is empty, or they are grieving, their Spirit says, "there is Perfect Life within you! In that life may be found infinite possibilities of delight and wonder! So now raise

---

[3] This is what is being described in Lesson Twelve of Emma Curtis Hopkins' teachings – that we are transcendent beings with transcendent powers. DeWaters is expanding on that lesson in this book.

your consciousness and enter! Behold what is already yours!" This Spirit is in all of us, calling each of us to look within and discover the rich life awaiting us.

Our lives have been limited by our past choices and understandings. It's as if, moving into a new house, we had limited ourselves to staying in the basement kitchen. The house had many other pleasant rooms, filled with light, but for some reason that we don't really understand and aren't even really aware of, we chose to spend all our days and nights in the kitchen.

At first it was fine—warm and safe, with easy access to necessities—but as dishes got dirty and we constantly experienced the mopping and cleaning and other kitchen chores that must be dealt with, this limited experience began to become unpleasant, a burden.

But why attack the brooms, mops, and dishes as if they were attacking us? There are plenty of other rooms to enjoy, instead of limiting our lives in this way! Simply by choosing to remain in the upper floors of our new house—in the library, the music room, the lovely bed rooms and sitting rooms—we would no longer be plagued by the conditions of the kitchen. We would find immediate and tremendous relief.

And so it is for us, here and now, and whenever we understand that we need not attack external circumstances or experiences. We realize we can "move to a higher room." By rising to a higher realm of thought, a new state of consciousness, we transcend those circumstances and dissolve those experiences. Thus, as our individual consciousness is uplifted, the whole world shifts. The universe of our being is uplifted as we ascend in thought.

OVERCOMING DISCORD

Entering into the state of consciousness that perceives, with the New Testament Jesus, that "You are the light!" we effortlessly put off all forms of darkness. As we understand and feel that we are immutable Life, we escape all the condition that are called disease and bondage. As we adopt and practice our true Reality, we put off all forms of limitation.

Like the music student who learns to avoid discordant sounds by understanding and practicing the fundamentals of harmony, we overcome and avoid discordant experiences by understanding and practicing our fundamental nature of perfect being.

People who believe themselves to be material beings must work within material limitations. People who believe themselves to be mental beings must work within mental limitations. But *those who no longer believe themselves to be material or mental beings enter into the state of consciousness in which they recognize themselves as what they truly are*: the immortal beingness that we call Spirit or God. They spontaneously leave the so-called material and mental states, and experience the state of Truth, Intelligence, Beauty, Joy, Harmony, and all the other qualities of the Spirit that we all are.

And how can Spirit be sick? How can Truth be false? How can Intelligence be ignorant? It's impossible. Therefore, as we realize this truth of our being—that we are Spirit beings, not material or mental beings—none of these conditions is possible.

So, since we know in our hearts that there is no possibility of distress or discordance in Spirit, then the way out of such experiences is to allow ourselves to *be* Spirit!

The time of attempting to overcome so-called conditions — of healing the sick, of restoring harmony — is ending. This new, higher vision is coming into view: the Science of Ascension; the science of *being* Truth; Wisdom, Intelligence, and all the qualities of Spirit; the science of spontaneously experiencing full health and blessedness as a result.

A NEW (TO US) FORM OF BEING

In the same way as a new technology quietly replaces the old, as the invention of the automobile led to a decline in the use of horse-drawn carts and carriages, and the development of computers and smartphones diminished handwriting and radios, the realization that we are Spirit moves us beyond the old concern about conditions like sin, sickness, and death into a new reality of activity and experience. As ignorance is overcome by Intelligence, human senses are overcome by Spiritual consciousness.

It's not a replacement of parts. Just as a butterfly isn't given wings by cutting off the caterpillar's feet, we don't receive heavenly harmony by cutting down or attacking our experience or environment. Rather, this glorifying Vision, this uplifting of individual consciousness into eternal Truth, this realization that we *are* the being of Truth, Joy, Peace, and Harmony is a new birth — our new and immortal birth.

Not only is this new body not a replacement, it's not an "add-on," either. As wings are not placed upon a caterpillar in an attempt to bring forth a butterfly, so the "light body" that we truly are is not placed upon a mortal, material body. The immaculate, spiritual body that is what we truly are already exists. It's in our spiritual DNA, just as the butterfly already exists in the caterpillar's physical DNA. It remains part of our potential, awaiting our effortless acceptance, our claim and willingness to allow it to become our experience. The truth of who and what we truly are awakens our inner Self to this new level of being. As we awaken, we are illuminated, enlightened, and the old dream of material existence is dispelled. Truth calls us to hear wondrous ideas. The light of understanding dispels the darkness of the dream world.

AT HAND

In the New Testament, Jesus reported that his vision saw the perfect universe at hand, the white fields harvested already, the radiant body prepared. "Inherit the kingdom... prepared for you," he told his followers.

The radiant Truth of our being, the Spirit, the Christ Self, having become our identity, the world around us must become heavenly. "In a twinkling of an eye we shall be changed." Then, as we realize that there is nothing *out there* to combat, confront, or even negate or dissolve, our spiritual expansion takes off, and all that has seemed to be disharmony simply disappears from our experience. No longer do we try to put new wine into the old, cracked wineskins, or to patch discordant circumstances with right ideas. Thought and vision that were once discordant are now united.

Our recognition and acceptance of our true, divine Self enables us to experience the abundance, happiness, and harmony that is already prepared and at hand. As we accept our immortality, the material body responds to our new way of thinking and feeling, showing forth our new state of consciousness as wonderful wellbeing in every aspect of our life and world.

BEYOND DARKNESS

"Come up higher!" is the call of the One Source of all being. Come up into a higher realization, where you'll experience illumination, and the transfiguration that results. The Science of Ascension is the process of uplifting our inner vision, and with it our state of consciousness, to a level where our old human beliefs and limitations are dissolved — and with them, the darkness of our previous way of living. As we move into fuller and fuller understanding, our consciousness is raised to higher and higher levels, and those old beliefs and limitations are eliminated proportionately.

The understanding that we *are* Life, Truth, and Love is the Light that shines eternally in us, whether we're aware of it or not. Indeed, no matter how deep one's mental darkness may seem, there is hidden in each one of us the glory of that Light, and it's because of that ever-present Light within that all may be delivered from any form of darkness. No dream of darkness can ever take away the reality of the presence of the glorious immortal Spirit that we all are.

The Hindu *Bhagavad Gita,* the Buddha's *sutras,* and the Christian New Testament, present a "way of salvation"[4] from our false beliefs, our beliefs in the reality of material limitation and bondage to material forms. That material sense of life must be put off; the false belief must yield to Truth, for in that Truth (in our Christ, Krishna, or Buddha nature) "all shall be made alive."

As this Science of Being dawns in our awareness, we release untrue beliefs, replacing them with

---

[4] The word "salvation" literally means, being saved from – we are saved from the consequences of our false beliefs and experience wholeness, fulfillment, completion instead.

spiritual realization that establishes, instead of the dream of material existence, the experience of our spiritual understanding. "You shall know the Truth and the Truth shall set you free," says Jesus the Nazarene, "Whoever focuses all their attention on Me becomes Me," says Krishna. They're telling us that, for anyone who takes in and retains a complete view of ideal being—perfect, infallible, changeless identity—the untrue sense of life is effortlessly put off; it vanishes.

A GRADUAL PROCESS

It happens in a sequence of experiences. The spiritual understanding is perceived and demonstrated gradually and gently, until we ultimately experience Jesus' promise: "be you therefore perfect."

Each of us emerges step by step from the belief that we are imperfect, material, and mortal to the recognition that we are Spirit: perfect, immortal beings having spiritual experiences in the dream of mortality. It's like the maturation process by which the child gradually disappears while the adult takes its place; the adult was always present in potential, though not initially visible. So it is that our human appearance gradually dissolves while the understanding and experience of the individual consciousness as immortal Spirit replaces it.[5]

We experience our true, Spirit identity and nature in direct proportion to the degree to which we understand and demonstrate the spiritual teachings of the ages. From the ancient scriptures of the Hindus, the

---

[5] This is what Henry Drummond is saying in his book *Spiritual Law in the Natural World,* included in the Library of Hidden Knowledge as *One Law*

Egyptians, and Sumerians, through the prophets of Israel, the teachings of the New Testament Jesus, and the alchemists of the European Enlightenment, we are told the solution is established in Eternity and available to all who practice the Science of Being. As the Christian apostle Paul put it, "When this mortal shall have put on immortality, then shall the saying that is written, 'Death is swallowed up in victory,' be brought to pass."

Each of us can live this way, from Spirit instead of from sense, by following the way that Jesus the Nazarene and the other great teachers taught and demonstrated. Just as we begin to solve a problem in arithmetic or mathematics knowing that the answer already exists and all we have to do is follow specific processes to find it, in the same way we know that the solution to material limitations exists, and we need only to follow specific processes to find that.

ALREADY PERFECT

So, since we are all *now* Spirit, perfect and immortal being, why does anyone speak of redemption, salvation, resurrection, or even ascension? The answer to that question is simple: we just haven't accepted it yet.

If we knew and had demonstrated full understanding of our redemption (from the dreams of the past), resurrection (from the belief in death), and ascension (into the state of consciousness in which none of those exist), we would not even be able think those words. Our True Being is never lost or fallen, and therefore is never resurrected; it's always alive and well in the reality of Spirit.

When we've achieved the full ascended state of consciousness, the body will no longer be visible to the human eye, but be deathless and immortal as the Light from which it has been formed. It's not transformed; it's changeless and immortal. *All that changes is the individual's belief or mistaken sense of being,* as it yields to the truth of its immortal reality through the Science of Ascension.

Referring again to the caterpillar, we see that the butterfly never crawls—that way of being has been replaced through the realization of the potential that was always there in the crawling caterpillar. It's the same for humanity: perfect being is always here, inherently and eternally. Our immortal being cannot be sick or sinful, and as we realize it, the old habits of thought—of sick ness, death, and other material limitations—cease automatically. We no longer crawl; we fly!

UNLIMITED BEING
       The Spirit that we truly are is not limited, not hampered by the dream of materiality. Our true, immortal being is free Spirit: omnipotent, omniscient, and omnipresent. It is timeless; not bound to the spacetime continuum of earthly human experience, but free in the Reality that is Heaven on Earth, which transcends space and time.

       The old phrase "overcome evil with good," is achieved effortlessly as we allow old beliefs of a sick or discordant body to be replaced with the True realization of our immortal Spirit body. We overcome the limitations of an unawakened state of consciousness with the awakened fire of true insight and perception. This transition—from an untrue sense of what our lives are to a new and true sense—is the resurrection.

       The awakening of our consciousness to our true Reality is awakening to the fact that we are Spirit, perfect and whole, and that there is no other being. We are all. Eternal. Whole. Complete. Nothing else exists.

This means that nothing that opposes our true immortal nature exists. Nothing that opposes Reality *can* exist; opposition is only the experience of a perception dulled by cultural beliefs and norms. So, also, is separation. Nothing exists outside the whole that is Spirit, so nothing and no one can be separate from the love, beauty, joy, comfort, harmony, peace, and all the other qualities that Sprit is.

REALIZATION

Truth, our true and ideal being and environment, is always here, without beginning and without end. Our eternal life is here as perfect Being; it's up to us to perceive and demonstrate the Reality, to realize it. And we experience that perfection in accordance with our individual understanding, faith, and acceptance.

Perfect being never changes, regardless of changing points of view; no misunderstanding or false belief can change the nature of Reality. So, as each of us begins to harmonize our beliefs with Reality, we must experience all the qualities of Spirit in our daily lives.

As each of us realizes the wholeness and completeness of our infinite Spirit nature, we see all our needs supplied, all our desires fulfilled, and all our ideals delivered.

"Be reconciled with God," is a promise of the Hebrew bible, the Christian Old Testament that must be fulfilled. Whether by suffering or by this Science, we must ultimately come to this reconciliation, this realization; we *will* come to our true Self. Truth *will* become known to us. As we reconcile ourselves with the existence of only One, one Spirit, one Substance, one

Power—as we accept this awareness, this vision, we begin to make that experience real in our experience; we come into Reality.

It could take years (lifetimes?) of suffering, overcoming step-by-step the falsehoods of cultural training, limited perception, and dulled consciousness. Or, we may study the path laid out by the Christ, the Buddha, the *yogis*, and the principles of alchemy—the Science of Ascension—to achieve this realization

A SCIENCE OF TRUTH

In the Christian New Testament, Jesus the Nazarene showed us how the dream of material existence may be broken, how the laws of that dream may be put aside, and how the experiences of sin, sickness, and death may be effortlessly annihilated. He showed us the path from mortality (our human sense) to our actual state, immortality (Spirit). He told us "You shall know the Truth," not after we have returned to our heavenly home, but now, in the dream of material existence. Here and now, Jesus said, is the time and place to learn and experience the Truth that delivers our freedom from the dream. Similarly, Krishna, Patanjali, and Gautama Buddha[6] tell us ways that we can discover the Truth of our immortal Self and so lift ourselves off the wheel of mortality.

This is not a science of moving up and out, but one of remaining still. It's not a science of putting on and off, but of recognition and acceptance of what is Real. This Science of Ascension is a practical demonstration, a science of seeing and demonstrating Reality in our own

---

[6] Krishna, in the *Bhagavad Gita* (c. 2500bce), Patanjali's Yoga aphorisms (c. 1600bce), and Gautama Buddha's Sutras (c.600bce).

being. It's a way above the path of suffering, above climbing and laborious effort. It's the Science of Fulfillment.

In a world of paths to walk, highways to drive, or planes to fly from one place to another, this is the science of being there without any process of traveling.[7] In a world in which the "prodigal son" must suffer and work his way back to his father's welcoming arms, this is the science of never having left the perfect Reality. It's the science of seeing that there is no requirement to return, that the only requirement is to know that we have never left, never wandered away except in a dream, and that we are, now and always, held in the embrace of perfect Life, Truth, Wholeness, and Love.

∞

SUMMARY POINTS

- Jesus the Nazarene is described as having practiced and taught a Science that not only enabled him to help and bless others on their plane of existence, but lifted him up into a reality of consciousness we call ascension.

- This Absolute Science shows us that, as we become aware of our true being as Spirit, we are no longer bound by the beliefs and misunderstandings of the material world, but are rising to the limitless state of being that is our true nature.

- In this state of consciousness, we don't just overcome undesirable conditions, those conditions no longer exist.

---

[7] Paramahansa Yogananda describes several instances of this ability in his book, *Autobiography of a Yogi.*

- People who believe themselves to be material beings must work within material limitations. People who believe themselves to be mental beings must work within mental limitations. But those who no longer believe themselves to be material or mental beings enter into the state of consciousness in which they recognize themselves as what they truly are.

- Each of us emerges step by step from the belief that we are imperfect, material, and mortal to the recognition that we are Spirit: perfect, immortal beings having spiritual experiences in the dream of mortality.

- As each of us begins to harmonize our beliefs with Reality, we must experience all the qualities of Spirit in our daily lives. As we realize the wholeness and completeness of our infinite Spirit nature, we see all our needs supplied, all our desires fulfilled, and all our ideals delivered.

- This Science of Ascension is a science of seeing and demonstrating Reality in our own being, a way above the path of suffering, above climbing and laborious effort: the Science of Fulfillment.

TO PONDER:

1. How have you thought of yourself and other people in the past? Are you a material being with a spirit? A spirit expressing as a human being? Are they? Are you part of something greater? If so, what? How?

2. If someone told you there is a step-by-step process for experiencing Heaven on Earth, would

you believe it was possible? If not, why not? If so, why?

3. What would it take for you to let go of old, limiting beliefs? What processes do you know about that would help overcome the things you were taught (or experienced) about yourself and the universe that keep you chained to material existence?

TO PRACTICE:

- Consider what part of your life does not feel heavenly right now. Does it seem familiar, has it or something like it happened in your life before?

- Remember the last time you experienced this, and see if you can remember previous times. Write them in a few words.

- Sit quietly with the memory for a while, and see what other experiences, or people, are associated with these experiences. Write their names and a few words about these experiences.

- Sit with what you've written; let your gaze flow over the words and names, feeling whatever feelings come up. If the feelings are intense, go somewhere where it's safe to express them (as in moving, shouting, throwing things, hitting pillows). If there are tears, let them flow.

- When you no longer feel the upset, get up and take a shower to release the feelings, and declare that they are no longer part of your world.

Chapter Two

Are We God?

To announce that we are Spirit means that we recognize and accept Spirit, often called God, as our real and true Self. The boldness of this statement has led many students to refrain from accepting the wonderful vision that we are, each of us is, Life, Truth, and Love. It has seemed prideful, even impertinent.

Our response to the question, "is man God?" must be that the question can't be answered as it stands, because there are too many interpretations of the words "man" and "God." When one hears the word "man," immediately the questions come up, "does this mean the real or the false man, the spiritual Self or the material body? Does it mean any person or just an adult male?" The same is true for the word "God." Some people see the word and imagine a person.

We can be great enough in nature, and hold a large enough vision, to recognize and accept Truth no matter who states it or what form of words they use. With insight we can penetrate any word formation to the meaning that may be hidden within it, then we can say the words differently, which makes it easy to confirm their truth and meaning.

Students, teachers, and writers could therefore avoid much confusion if they would substitute more specific terms. Using, instead, the words for the divine qualities—Truth, Spirit, Self, Reality, etc.—we can avoid such misunderstandings. Asking the question in a more precise way, as, for example, "Are we Life, Truth, and Love?" the words do not need to be interpreted and the question can be answered satisfactorily.

IMAGE? LIKENESS?

Writers of the Christian and Hebrew Bibles, and some modern teachers of metaphysics, speak of "man" as an "image," or "likeness," "idea," or "manifestation." Are they saying that I, myself, am merely an image or likeness of something greater?

Truly not so! No one having experienced a baptism of the fire of insight consider themselves to be mere images of the whole. Their experience tells them that they are infinitely more than an image, greater than a manifestation or idea, they have felt themselves *as* the whole. As we penetrate more deeply, though, opening our vision more fully, we soon see just what it is that is an image, just what is called "man — the image of God." It is the body. The body is an image that enacts, portrays, expresses, and manifests the invisible qualities, health, life, strength, power, intelligence, substance, and reality of individual consciousness. *The body is the manifestation, the expression, of individualized consciousness.*

INSEPARABLE

So "man," an individual body, is the visible embodiment, and "God" is the invisible Life bringing forth that body. They are clearly different forms of being, *and yet they are inseparable.*

We would not say that the body in the mirror and the body facing the mirror are the same being. We know that the body in the mirror is an image or reflection of the body outside it and only appears to have the same form, The two are not the same, but they are inseparable — the image cannot exist without the body in front of it, and the body does not exist without casting images on reflective surfaces.

In the same way that the body must (can't not) cast a reflection, Spirit must express a manifestation. The body is the individualized Spirit in form; it is how Spirit acts, expresses, and manifests. We know that they are inseparable: manifester and manifestation; Spirit and embodiment; ideal and form.

ONE BEING, ONE BODY

And yet to consider oneself only an image or manifestation is to ignore the Truth. Our individual being comprises both consciousness and body; it is both Spirit, as Life-Truth-Wisdom-Beauty, and the form of Spirit's expression.

We must remember that there is only ONE being and this one is ALL. There is no being outside this ONE. All being is Spirit, God. All life is Reality, God. All knowledge is Truth, God.

This means that our Self or individualized Spirit, the I AM of each of us, is more than a mere image or manifestation. It is the one being that is All. It is the one Life, Intelligence, and Substance. As the great Islamic poet Rumi has said "you are not a drop in the ocean; you are the ocean in a drop." As Jesus says in the New Testament, "I am the Way, the Truth, and the Life," and Krishna, in the *Bhagavad Gita* tells us. "I am the birthless, the deathless, Lord of all that breathes. I seem to be born; it is only seeming."

As most of us began our study of metaphysics, we found it easy to consider ourselves children of God, sons and daughters of an omnipotent Father. It made sense that all of the limited natural world is an offspring, or expression, of the Infinite. We were bridging from the cultural idea of separation to a sense of connection.

We would have been amazed, then, to be told of the true magnificence and omnipotence of our being, but how could Intelligence and its idea be divided? How could consciousness, Spirit, and its embodiment be separated? Of course, it cannot be.

As there is no separation, Life, Being, is One, and this One is all inclusive. The universe, including all of nature and humanity, must therefore be the body of the One Life and Truth that we call God.

The Self can be none other than the one Reality, for there is nothing else to be. We are both Creator and creation; both Intelligence and idea; both Self and body. And this unit is indivisible, inseparable, irresistible, everlasting, and eternal.

Don't be afraid to step out into the great sea of this understanding. Everything that is Real, true, perfect, whole, is included in the all that is ONE. The ONE is universal; it is the Source (called, in the New Testament and other traditions, Father); and the individual Self (called, in the New Testament and other traditions, the Son).[8]

RELATING TO THE BODY

It's curious that an understanding of the nature of the body is one of the last revelations to come to many, though it's among the first questions that a student of metaphysics asks. The thought of what the body truly is seems to be one of those blind spots in learning.

Many of us have discovered that we don't understand something until we come to the point in our lives

---

[8] *A Course In Miracles,* whose narrator calls himself Jesus the Christ, says that all that has been created, including all people, taken together can be called the "Son of God."

where we *can* understand it. We may read or hear the right answer to a question many times but not be able to take it in; the meaning escapes us. Then, years later, when we are ready, the answer presents itself again, and now, how different our response! We hail it with great joy! The answer has always been there but we could not perceive its Truth.

It's been said by wise teachers over the ages that as we approach Truth, so Truth approaches us. So, now, let's claim the highest Truth we can imagine. Let's open up that blind spot in our awareness and accept that our body, our real, divine body, is the perfect embodiment of Wisdom, Intelligence, Life, Substance, Being.

Now some may feel that they must not hope for or expect so much, that it might be safer to remain a "son" than to acknowledge being the "Father." Yet neither the Judeo-Christian scriptures nor the Hindu and Buddhist traditions support that notion. Quoting Psalm 82 in the Hebrew Bible, Jesus asks, "Have ye not read that ye are gods?" and he says, "Great is your holiness... You are the light of the world!" Krishna identifies us with the Source of all, saying "the individual self is Brahman mistakenly identified with matter (*prakriti* in Sanskrit)." And the *yogis* and Gautama Buddha invite people to enter into a state of consciousness in which they no longer misidentify themselves as separate, material beings.

We assume a responsibility — and often a very heavy one — if we take ownership of this body as if it were outside our consciousness. If, for instance, the body were to feel weak and sick, one's belief might be that it should be fixed so that it will look and act right again, as we do with an automobile. Thinking this way, one becomes personally accountable for the health, harmony, and maintenance of one's body.

Yet this is not how the universe works! Do you recall from the New Testament, how Jesus brought attention to the growing of a lily? How beautiful its body? How fragrant its perfume? And yet how totally unconscious of its beauty! He told his followers to "...consider the lilies of the field. They do not toil; neither do they spin..." The lily assumes no responsibility for its well-being, yet behold its beauty of form and being.

Then he reminded his listeners that they—all humanity—are placed in a much higher position than any lily; we have a form and a body far superior to that of a lily planted in the earth. Your body is not fixed in the ground, subject to whatever comes to it.

Indeed, our Self does not have a body that can be destroyed, or is subject to age, limitation, and disease. How could a spiritual being become weak and weary, old and crippled? Unthinkable!

Shall we stop clothing and caring for the body? Not at all. But we can change our perception of the body. We can come into a higher understanding of what body must be, thereby blessing not only our bodies and our sense of self, but the whole world.

> One day, a man was resting under a tree, feeling tired and wishing he were not fatigued. As he sat there the thought came to him that he would be much happier if he didn't have to care about his body. "Yes," he thought, "that's it. Why should I be compelled to think of it? I really know so little about the body anyhow. I do not understand how I live nor how I sleep in the body. I don't understand how my blood circulates or my food digests. In fact, now that I see it, I know little or nothing about the body..."
> His next thought came as a sudden insight. "Well, then, why

have any unnecessary care or worry over it at all? Can there be any body except the body of Truth? Is there anything besides Truth?"

"What a wonderful thought!" he mused. "Why shouldn't Truth be my body? Am I consciousness and body?" An inner Voice seemed to reply, "You are not dual. You are one. Whatever there is of you must be the ALL of you. You are Myself; I am Yourself." The Voice went on, "This is one Whole, one ALL, one being, one action, one form, one Life." The man had been caught up by Spirit, and now there came to him an illumined sense of joy, uplift, and harmony.

Haven't we all noticed that when the body is perfectly well and normal that it causes us no concern — that, in fact, we quite forget it for a time? It's as if it were a shadow, going along with us wherever we wish to go, while we are totally unaware of it.

Now think about a dream. Perhaps you dream that you are traveling with a group of friends on a cruise ship. You can plainly see the great ship and watch the white waves. You look at your friends, see the color of their hair, what they're wearing, and you can easily know who is who. And you're doing all this without conscious effort, no consideration of whether you or they are mental or physical beings.

In that dream you could be sitting at a table, enjoying a marvelous meal without it ever occurring to you that you have a stomach or could have indigestion. You can run up and down the stairs without effort; you sing and talk and dance with glorious joy and abandon.

Your body is not in any way a consideration in your dream. Although you do all these things with the body, you're barely aware of it. In fact, you're totally unconscious of it as it accompanies you throughout the unfolding of the dream.

Similarly in your daily life, you perform many tasks, engage in many activities effortlessly, totally unconscious of your body. You awaken in the morning with no idea of how you do so; it's simply something that happens every day. You have a meal without making the digestive process happen. You breathe and the air moves into and through your body, touching every cell, without you making it happen. You go to sleep at night without any idea of how that happens. Indeed, when you try to make yourself sleep, you fail more often than not.

When our bodies are radiant with the glow of perfect health, we often forget about them entirely. The more health, the less thinking about the body. We set our intention and the body accompanies us — as does our shadow or our reflection in the glass.

Now this does not mean that we have no body; rather, it's a reminder that we are not subject to any of the physical processes of the body, not responsible for making any of those processes happen, and ideally have no attachment to the body at all.

LETTING GO

So, dear reader, are we ready to let go of that sense of attachment and responsibility coming with a personal sense of body? Are we willing to be "absent from the body and present with our Lord?"

Have no fear that in letting go of attachment to the body you might lose the body itself. Quite the contrary. By letting go of a sense of attachment to and responsibility for the body you form a true understanding of the body in relation to your Self.

It's wonderful, really. To be willing to NOT heal or change the body is to find oneself on the road to a body that is not sick, limited, or changeable[9] — a body immortal, eternal, and everlasting. A body *immune*.

We know that if anyone believes their body to be material in nature, then their body is subject to material laws and processes. But if we lay no claim to a separate, external, or physical body at all, wouldn't we be out of the reach of disease, distress, or any form of limitation, altogether?

Consider this question slowly, meditatively. It's momentous.

We know that when we find the true idea of anything, old, false ideas drop away automatically. Keeping this in our awareness, it makes sense to consider *why* our bodies cannot be sick, and so to see that we can have no false body.

ONE REALITY, INDIVISIBLE

Since Reality is all that is, then all that exists is Reality. Therefore, whatever the body is, it must be Reality, in and of Reality. Life and form are one; Spirit and body are one; Cause and effect are one[10] — now, always, *and forever*.

Truth is not any form; Truth is all form. Being is not divided into forms; Being is all form.

None of us can go out of Life because we ARE Life. We cannot go out of Health because we ARE Health. We cannot be outside our heavenly existence, for we ARE

---

[9] This is the essence of Emma Curtis Hopkins' practice for lesson 4, in which we covenant with Spirit to do all things through the body for the good of all, and we do nothing to maintain it.

[10] Ralph Waldo Emerson, in his essays on Spiritual Law, says that the effect is *in* the cause; the flower is in the seed; the result is in the action; the outcome is in the thought (available in Ruth Miller's Library of Hidden Knowledge volume: *Natural Abundance).*

the Heaven we have been seeking. We cannot be a soul having a body, because body and soul are one; both are Spirit. We cannot be separated, divided, in any way, for *we are complete and indivisible Being.*

Form is the expression — as necessary and eternal and indestructible as the Self which is expressed.

Consider the ascended body of Jesus the Nazarene; presented in so many portraits over the millennia in so many ways. Yet it must be unchanging.

Recently, some artists have experienced Jesus' presence in their lives, and have portrayed what they experienced.[11] And engineers have reconstructed the negative image on the Shroud of Turin into a positive image, which another artist as made into a portrait.

20th century images of Jesus the Nazarene

by 12-year-old Akiane   by Glenda Green   Yogananda's preferred image

Negative image   reconstruction   portrait
                      from the Shroud of Turin

---

[11] While there are thousands of depictions of Jesus of Nazareth, who is said to have resurrected his body and shown up in the world many times since, two paintings have been done in the past 50 years where the painters experienced a being emerging in their studio to sit for painting, teaching them the ways of the Christ.

As form in the expression of Spirit must be indestructible, these images must be similar — allowing for differences in the artists' style and perception. Perceiving form is like the fact that when we hear a voice on the phone, we know that we are hearing the person, not some entity living in the phone; the phone is just the mode of transmission. The body is Truth in expression, as the voice over the phone is the person in expression.

It's the same with spirit and body; Creator and creation. In the book of Genesis we read that Spirit created form — as matter, energy, and information; as stars, planets, water, land, plants and animals — and called it Good.[12]

As Good is another name for God, we can easily say then that *all form is Spirit made manifest.*

ONE SPIRIT, INDIVIDUALIZED

This is not pantheism; that would be saying each form has its own spirit. This is not reincarnation, either; that is saying that a soul takes on many forms, in different times and spaces. This is, rather, the emerging understanding among scientists and mystics that is called panpsychism or panentheism: *Spirit (or, in scientific terms, consciousness, intelligence) is present everywhere; it's limitless, infinite, eternal, coming into form.*

The individualization of Spirit is what we call Self, and Self is always experiencing infinite forms of matter, energy, and information through direct apprehension.

---

12 Thomas Troward, in his *The Creative Process in the Individual*, describes the act of creation as Spirit contemplating its own Beingness, and in doing so, expressing that Beingness in form (available in Ruth Miller's Library of Hidden Knowledge volume: *The Creative Power of Thought.*).

The mode of expression is what we call body — experiencing and expressing as matter, energy, and information through the limitations of senses and stored memories. They are inseparable aspects of the One Being that we all are.

Yes, we, each of us and all of us, are that One. The One shining in the star, sparkling in the water, blooming in the rose, soaring in the bird. The One expressing in all life, all beings, as one Being. Not only do we all share the atoms that formed in the stars, we all share the very Beingness that became those atoms.

One Being, one all. The One, all height and no height; the One, all time and no time; the One, all form and no form; the One, all language and no language; the One, all motion and no motion; the One *indescribable, unspeakable, incomparable!*[13] And the One that is being and creating All That Is says to each and all of us:

> You are my infinite Self; all that I am, you are; all that is mine is also yours.
>
> You are not a thing that has a soul;[14] you are soul as Self, eternal being. Being is not something that has body; Being includes body. Your form is eternal idea made visible; you, therefore, are immortal Being in immortal form.
>
> Your essence, your Self, is Being, eternal. Your mode of expression is Being in form, immortal body.

---

[13] Lao Tse tells us, in the *Tao te Ching*, that "the Tao that can be named is not the Tao." Daniel Nahmod's song "One Power" says it's "indescribable, yet we speak of it with every word we say."

[14] DeWaters calls the eternal Self, the individualization of Spirit that is the core of each person, as soul. Because today's psychologists, like Thomas Moore in his *Care of the Soul*, define soul as the combined emotions, thoughts, and memories unique to each per son, we are using the term Self to describe our spiritual essence, instead.

EXPERIENCING REALITY

And so we speak the great formula, the "Lord's Prayer" or "Our Father," in a whole new way, with a whole new understanding:

Oh, our One Source-Self, Blessed is Our Being! Our domain is come! Our will is always done—on this earth as heaven! We give each day of Our daily supply and We joyously forgive all debts and debtors, trespasses and trespassers, knowing that all is, and we are, all One.

We are never left in a temptation to believe in the appearance of forms, and so are delivered from every distress; for the power and glory of All That Is expresses through Us and as Us in this great realm of being, forever!

Insight, inspiration, our spiritual vision, shows us the multiverse in all its glory, and we see clearly, across space and time, the spiritual nature of all that is.

This spiritual sight is "the light that shines in the darkness" showing us order instead of disorder, harmony instead of discord, unity instead of division. In that vision, focused on the spiritual reality within and beyond the material, evil is nonexistent; duality is swallowed up in the same way as turning on a light dissolves the shadow. All is One and it is Good.

We focus our vision on "the new heaven and new earth"—no longer separate states, but joined in our experience —as symbolized by the foursquare new Jerusalem described in John's Revelation. To do so, it's helpful to speak words that are attuned to that higher order of being. So, with each breath, we can repeat such words as

eternity	infinity	freedom	omniscience
omnipotence		omnipresence	
everlasting peace		harmony	resurrection
	ascension		

We let the cares of the falsifying senses go and relax in the Reality of the One that Is all Love, all Light, all Peace; we let the words and worries of the senses go and listen only to the high Voice of Spirit.

No More Illusion

Illusion is not in the thing itself, but in our concept of that thing. When we interpret our experience through the veil of space, time, and personality (culturally trained neural network in the brain, also called ego), is it any wonder that we perceive duality, division, relativity?

In the Christian bible, the perfection of creation is depicted in the beginning (the garden in the book of Genesis) and in the end (the new Jerusalem described in John's Revelation), without blemish, radiantly reflective as the purest mirror — from beginning to end, perfect, whole, and complete. As in mathematics, the integers two plus two are always four; perfect, whole, and complete, so it is with Life. Life is whole, complete, without any variation, changeless always, in every situation. Truth is Reality; you can't change it. And you are Reality, for there is nothing else for you to be!

SPEAKING WORDS OF TRUTH

Recently, the author was awakened in the middle of the night to treat a sudden, serious illness.[15] Immediately, not even really awake, she said "Tell him two and two are four." That message was not at once accepted by the caller, as it didn't seem spiritual, but the author was being guided by Spirit and insisted that it

---

[15] DeWaters was a Christian Science practitioner who went off on her own as she saw limitations in that teaching (as did Joel Goldsmith, later, as well). She is relating a personal experience here.

was what was needed. The message was delivered, and the next day the healed man came to call and comment on the strangeness of what he'd been told.

"Did you not find that you went immediately to sleep and that your attack vanished?" He acknowledged it was so. The words of truth established the Reality of Life in his awareness, undoing the temporary falsehood of distress.

This is an excellent example of the power of the spontaneous treatment—it leaps over words, transcending dimensions, declaring what is so in perfect harmony with the individual at that moment. So, in treating others, don't feel you must "dress up" your words of faith; Truth spoken with authority from the heart is the power that transcends dreams of illusion.

Indeed, one should never hesitate to speak from an illumined state of consciousness in the moment, for those words are the fire that consumes illusions; they are the Power that restores true Reality in one's experience.

$$\infty$$

SUMMARY POINTS

- The question, "is man God?" can't be answered as it stands, because there are too many interpretations of the words "man" and "God."

- Asking "Are we Life, Truth, and Love?" the words do not need to be interpreted to answer the question.

- What is called "man—the image of God" is the body.

- The body is the individualized Spirit in form; it is how Spirit acts, expresses, and manifests.

- We cannot be a soul having a body, because body and soul are one; both are Spirit, individualizing as the Self.

- The Self can be none other than the one Reality, *for there is nothing else to be.*

- None of us can go out of Life because we ARE Life. We cannot go out of Health because we ARE Health.

- We cannot be outside our heavenly existence for we ARE the Heaven we've been seeking.

- This spiritual insight is "the light that shines in the darkness" showing us order instead of disorder, harmony instead of discord, unity instead of division.

- Focused on the Truth of the spiritual reality within and beyond the material, evil is nonexistent; duality is swallowed up in the same way as turning on a light dissolves the shadow. All is One and it is Good.

- Truth spoken with authority from the heart is the power that transcends dreams of illusion.

TO PONDER:

1. How can it be that if we no longer claim a separate, external, or physical body at all, we would be out of the reach of disease, distress, and any form of limitation?

2. What would it take to stop thinking of the body

as something you're responsible for, that needs care and maintenance, and to start experiencing it as Spirit made manifest? How does Jesus' references to "lilies of the field" relate?

3. In saying a treatment for others, have you felt you must "dress up" your words of faith? How does Truth spoken with authority from the heart transcend dreams of illusion?

4. What does it feel like to speak from an illumined state of consciousness in the moment? As you align your awareness as your Self, what words come to you as the fire that consumes illusions, the Power that restores Reality in one's experience?

TO PRACTICE:

- Try taking some time each day to speak words that are attuned to that higher order of being; with each breath, repeat such words as eternity, infinity, freedom, everlasting peace, omniscience, omnipotence, omnipresence, harmony, resurrection, ascension.

- Pay attention to your body as you do so: does it change?

- Pay attention to your relationships and activities; is there a difference?

CHAPTER THREE

THE SCIENCE OF BEING

In the 1870s, Mary Baker Eddy, founder of the Christian Science church, wrote in her textbook:

That we are Spirit, and Spirit is God, is undeniably true... The final understanding that we are Spirit must come... At present we know not what we are, but this is certain: that we shall be Love, Life, and Truth, when we understand them.[16]

The belief that we are human beings, subject to a material world, has resulted in all the limitation and discord present on the Earth today. Is it possible that the understanding that we are soul, Spirit, the essence of All that Is — the recognition and acceptance of the actuality of our being — is the truth that will set us free from the consequences of that false be lief?

In the New Testament, we see that Jesus the Nazarene said "I, if I be lifted up, will draw all men to me." When Truth, as our Buddha nature, Krishna, or the Christ (which is to say Spirit in form), is lifted up in anyone's vision, they experience a new recognition and understanding, such that the whole universe takes on a new glory. So it is that anyone, by identifying their self as Life, Love, Spirit, automatically rises to new heights of being. This means that, when Jesus said "you must be born again," he was referring to the process of letting go of old beliefs and replacing them with this greater understanding, this new glory, which is a form of rebirth.

---

[16] From *Science and Health with Key to the Scriptures,* written originally in 1876 by Mary Baker Eddy.

JESUS THE NAZARENE: EXEMPLIFYING THE WAY

The New Testament gospels tell us that Jesus the Nazarene infuriated the Jewish leadership by claiming and acting on his deity. They saw him as a man like themselves and considered his teaching and actions to be blasphemy, not realizing that he was claiming the spiritual power that he used to heal the sick and raise the dead not just for himself, but for all of us, including the scholars who mocked him.

Those gospel stories describe Jesus as the ideal Self, God in the flesh, and in those stories, he said that whatever is true of him is also true of all of us. We see his great love for humanity prompting him to demonstrate to the very end his absolute understanding of unchangeable Life and Being—to show clearly to all that he held the keys to a heavenly life, regardless of any appearance to the contrary.

So, by studying the life and teachings of Jesus the Nazarene, we begin to claim our own power, our own Life, Truth, and Love. Studying his story touches our hearts and awakens our love. As he is quoted as saying: "No one comes to the Source except through (the Christ Spirit in) me." As we identify ourselves with the Christ Spirit in Jesus, we identify ourselves with the Life, Truth, and Power that is our true Self.

AVAILABLE TO ALL

The term Christ is not a name. It comes from the Greek word for "highest, best," which is the root of the English word 'crest." In Sanskrit and Hindi, Krishna is also used as a name, but refers to beingness that is fully aware of its oneness with the source; we are told, in the ancient text called *Bhagavad Gita ("Song of God")*, that by focusing our full attention on him we can become him, and so experience the myriad forms of divinity that Krishna is in our own selves.

Other teachers provide insights, as well, and help us achieve the same awakened state. Lao Tse (which means "ancient master"), writing several hundred years before the New Testament, tells us that we are the Tao, the infinite unnamable lifeforce and source of all that is. Gautama Buddha, also living several hundred years before the gospels, was the first documented "Awakened One" (the meaning of the term Buddha) in India, and was a great teacher and miracle worker who has helped millions let go of old beliefs and begin to experience their true nature, which is called by his followers our "Buddha nature."

Whatever these ancient teachers claimed for themselves, they claimed for us all. They all say, as Jesus is quoted as saying, "… the glory which You (my Source and Spirit) have given me I have given them … that they all may be one in us… that they may be perfect in one…"

So the Christ/Krishna/Buddha essence of each of us says, "I am Life. I am Truth. I am the Source of all. I am God."

THE SCIENCE

Given that understanding, shall we identify ourselves as limited human beings or as the unlimited, free, flawless Spirit that is our true nature?

This Science of Ascension is the path by which we can achieve the essential understanding that helps us make that shift.

Through this science, a new understanding of Reality is moving across the world. Soon it will be perceived and understood that life is not a problem for each person to solve, but that the solution has already been reached and it is now up to us to accept that solution, and experience the joyful glory that comes with it.

Through this science we see that, for example, our health is not coming to us, but is already here. Insofar as we accept that fact, we experience perfect wellbeing. It's not that heaven is coming to us, or that Earth is coming to a heavenly state, but that "heaven is at hand," already present and all around us, ready for us to accept it, to shift our consciousness and allow ourselves to experience it, moment by moment.

We must reach a positive state of agreement and acceptance in order to experience the Reality that is already present. "Agree with your adversary quickly," Jesus told his followers, "...nothing shall in any way hurt you." "United with me you shall overcome all difficulties by my grace," said Krishna to his student, Arjuna, "lay down all duties in me, your refuge. Fear no longer...".

Just as Moses told the Israelites to stand by the Red Sea "and behold your salvation" from the Egyptians, we, right where we are, stand still and behold our salvation from all distress. We acknowledge it. We accept it. We celebrate it as we behold it unfolding for us—as the Israelites did after their safe crossing.

We understand that Spirit is infinite and all, and Reality cannot be separated or divided, so we must be the Reality we have sought. We know that this Reality, this Spirit, cannot be limited; cannot be harmed, cannot be afraid. Therefore, we are free of such things.

THE POWER OF REALIZED VISION

Anyone with this understanding, this vision, must see only good, not as the opposite of evil, but as omnipresent goodness, just as "to the pure all things are pure."

The same with health. Anyone with this understanding, this vision of being, sees health, not as the absence of sickness, but as ever-present wholeness. Those who live by this understanding speak only of Reality and so preach Reality to those who are captive to matter and limited thoughts. As light kindles light, so our recognition and praise of the Christ/ Krishna/Buddha Self brings forth a radiance of mind that cannot be deceived, a glory of body that cannot be sick. In this understanding, the One Mind, the Christ mind, is our mind.

The New Testament gospels make this clear:

- Did Lazarus come forth from the tomb as a living being because Jesus called him? No, Jesus called him because he knew Lazarus was a living being.

- Was it because of lack of food that Jesus supplied baskets full of bread and fish to the thousands who gathered to listen to him? No, it was because he saw an abundance of food that the thousands were fed.

- Was it because the man's arm was withered that Jesus told him to stretch it forth? No, it was because he knew the man's arm was perfect and whole.

- Was Jesus in opposition to the storm as he walked upon the waves? Or in condemnation of the woman at the well who had lived with several different men when he offered her living water? No, it was because he moved with the nature of water and knew the perfection of the woman that he did these things.

- He functioned in unity, in oneness, in heaven here on Earth, now.

The gospels relate that, as Jesus became the Christ, his vision—his very self—was atonement, and he showed us a path of atonement and unity with each other and with the Source. Born into our form and condition, he was visible to all as "one of us" and gradually showed us his — and our — true nature. He unified, he welcomed, he blessed, he fulfilled, he agreed, and in the process, he redeemed all humanity from our perceived separateness. To those who had the vision of Reality he was the Christ, risen into full Reality, out of the limited appearances of this world.

Likewise, Krishna showed his student, Arjuna, the path of atonement and unity. He encouraged Arjuna to focus on him, on Krishna's power and presence, and then simply go through the motions that the historical moment he found himself in required, without concern for the results. And Lao Tse invites his readers to allow, be unified with, and discover the power of simply being who and what we truly are, regardless of the circumstances around us — thus rising above, and even transforming, those circumstances.

NOT OF THIS WORLD

In the gospel stories, Jesus is said to leave the appearances of this world alone. "I walk in it, but I am not of it." He was telling us he wasn't affected by the world around him, that while he seemed to be living and eating and walking in our world, he was actually eating other food, walking in another reality. He was living a heavenly existence in a world he was constantly explaining: what he called the "kingdom of heaven."

In the *Tao te Ching*, the Hindu *Bhagavad Gita*, Rumi's Sufi poetry, and the Buddhist *Sutras*, we hear similar encouragements.

In the *Bhagavad Gita* Krishna tells us,

...when the ego-sense of self and heart are freed from delusion, united with Brahman [the Source-conscious ness of all that is] ... when sight and taste and sound are abandoned without regretting... when one eats but little, curbing speech, thoughts, and body, ever focusing on the Truth that is Brahman, and full of compassion... through this knowledge [that one] enters at once into my Being.

And the Buddha says,

The *Tathágata* [one who has come and gone] does not seek salvation in austerities, but neither does he for that reason indulge in worldly pleasures, nor live in abundance. The *Tathágata* has gained the knowledge of the Middle Way which leads to insight, which leads to wisdom, which conduces to calm, to knowledge, to Supreme Enlightenment, to Nirvana.

Rumi, the Sufi sage, tells us,

Stop looking for something out there and begin seeking within. ... Why get involved with a hag like the world? You know what it will cost. Don't strive so much to complete your worldly affairs; don't strive in any affair that is not sacred... No, but by burying your own self in the One... buried in your love of the Beloved... in that breath yours may be replenished.

THREE STAGES OF REALIZATION

Unlike the priests in temples, these teachers did not provide an outer path to the state of consciousness that we call atonement. Instead, they offered an inner way, a way to enter a new state of consciousness. They encouraged three steps along the way:

1. Recognize that the world, the universe, is not a set of objects "out there," but is instead an image, a hologram, of our thoughts, feelings, treasured memories, and vision.

2. Recognize that any belief in so-called evil, or

distress of any kind, is the result of a lack of understanding and realization of the fullness, wholeness, completion, and unity of every being and all that is.

3. Fill our individual awareness with, immerse our consciousness in, a full, clear vision of Reality as ever-present, thus becoming "reborn" into our full, Spirit Self and recognizing all beings as immortal, perfect, and whole.

Through this process, they tell us, we gradually awaken; we no longer walk in delusion, but in Reality, and experience only the good that Is, everywhere.

WHICH CREATION?

We read in the book of Genesis that "God saw everything that was made and, behold, it was good." All manifestation is proclaimed perfect, whole, and good, including all forms of life.

Then Genesis mentions a second creation, following the first. What can this be but an interpretation of the first? What was complete and whole is now seen through worldly, materialist eyes — imperfectly and incompletely instead of perfect, whole, and complete; darkly instead of clearly, as in an unpolished mirror.

Moses, the composer of both stories[17], speaks of a "mist" surrounding this second creation, and tells us that Adam, the man who was formed in the process, fell

---

[17] While tradition has it the Hebrew Prophet Moses (also called Moshe) is the author of Genesis and the next 4 books of the Bible (also called *Torah* or the Pentateuch), historians now understand that they are compilations of stories that the Hebrew people gathered and shared in their wanderings through southwestern Asia.

into a dream, from which he never, through the rest of the story, awakens.

A spiritual being sees and knows Truth. The true Self sees its own power, dominion, joy, peace, wonder, infinity, eternity, wholeness, and invariableness. So, as we know the Truth of our being, we know also the true nature of all that is; like Jesus, we call attention to the perfect world, the first Creation, that is now in our midst.

GRADUAL UNDERSTANDING

Individual consciousness interprets the perfect Creation by degrees, and as vision enlarges, each of us beholds more and more completely the perfection of the whole. Where once humanity was limited by the body's physical abilities, imagination has allowed us to transcend those limitations. Where once we saw human error and distress, we gradually begin to see the heavenly creation that was declared Good, instead.

Take, for example, our material modes of travel. Instead of being instantly where we intend to be (as has been demonstrated by yogis and saints, as well as Jesus and Krishna) the idea of walking and being carried came into being—which over time, evolved into riding, then being pulled on a cart or carriage, which became the current forms of automobile. Then the idea of the airplane emerged and was developed, so that, today, the highest concept of instantaneous arrival is the nonstop flight from city to city, preceded and followed by rides in automobiles.

With a little more clearing of the mist, or lifting of the veil, an even faster and more easily constructed device will be developed, and then someone will find a way to carry their own body quickly wherever they wish to go. Then, finally, the great light will dawn that each of us may move to exactly where we intend to be by the simple action of thought and will.

We can say, therefore, that the great advancement of invention that is occurring in so many areas of our material lives today is happening only because of great advancement in spiritual vision. Multitudes of people, all over the world, are applying their vision of Reality, of the perfect Creation, to transcend the limited beliefs of the past. So, day by day, humanity is approaching that state of being, that ultimate Vision, which, the New Testament gospels tell us, Jesus the Nazarene offered us so many years ago.

SPIRITUAL UNDERSTANDING LEADS TO HEAVENLY EXPERIENCE

Both the mental and material planes are controlled by our spiritual understanding. The spiritual vision of oneself as free, flawless being blesses the mental plane, changing the brain. Literally, the neural networks in the brain, which form our constant stream of thought, begin to take on new structures. We begin to have new thought patterns, and with each new thought pattern, we begin to see new ideas of what is possible.

Spiritual vision blesses our lives on the material plane, as well. As we lift our vision the people around us appear differently: they eat, dress, and act in more complete alignment with their true nature, constantly rising from glory to glory. Then our connectedness is experienced as never before. We become aware that hearts are blending across the globe, regardless of geographical or cultural barriers.

Since the world that we experience is a reflection of our consciousness, then to judge any aspect of the world as not good is to judge one's own thoughts and feelings as "not good." Isaiah the prophet said, "Woe unto them who call evil good and good evil, that put darkness for light and light for darkness." One who knows the Allness of good, which must be so because of the Allness of the divine qualities that we call God's omnipresence, doesn't preach to others about the presence or absence of evil in the world, but about the need to change one's thoughts to experience good.

The word is repent, which is to say, rethink, to think in a new way. Repent of what? Rethink the belief that what we perceive, including any appearance of not good, has any reality or power. Since our perceptions are based on past programming in the brain, only when we "rewire" that programming, think in a new way -- only when we feel and accept the allness and everpresence of good -- can we experience and understand the nothingness of all discord and disharmony.

OUR HEAVENLY EXPERIENCE

Whatever we accept as reality, as power, as presence, constitutes our world at that moment — which is to say that the world we experience exists *in* us; it is our consciousness outpicturing around us. As people understand the omnipresence of the good that is the only Reality, they discard any untrue beliefs and *refuse the temptation to perceive* anything other than good in their lives and in their world.

Here's an example of how this works:

A woman on a busy street in the city suddenly noticed a great crowd of people blocking traffic. Moving along to see the cause of the commotion, her eyes reported an accident: two vehicles had come together, a man lay underneath them and a horse was acting out its distress.

Now, as this woman looked, this panorama of excitement, commotion, and accident was reported to her external vision, but she heard a Voice very close at hand. It was the voice of her inner world, and it said: "Never mind what these people are seeing, what are *you* seeing?"

"Yes! What am I seeing?" she asked herself, "Why, I'm seeing Heaven!" she cried joyously, unconsciously moving out of the crowd. "There are no accidents in my world! In my world there is eternal changeless order and delight."

The incident was wiped from her awareness as she happily continued on her way.

Several weeks later she happened to meet a friend who, not knowing she had been near the scene, began describing it to her and said, "The strangest thing of all happened. Suddenly it all seemed to be over. The people seemed to be on their way without any departure; the horse involved became quiet; the trampled man stood up refusing assistance, and the havoc and excitement changed to order and normalcy – like a miracle."

We all see the so-called outer world according to our own spiritual awakening.

As individual perception coalesces with True Consciousness, false belief—with its associated experience—slips from the patterns of thought as a dream, and manifestation is perceived in its true light. Jesus cast out false beliefs because of the awareness of Truth in himself.

This is spiritual healing; the brain is now aligned with our true mind, Spirit, and any erring or discordant condition that seems to manifest is dissipated by the living Truth, the Christ/Krishna/Buddha state of consciousness. Experiencing such healing proves to us the unreality of all discord and limitation.

So, in which world are we living? Are we living in a material world, subject to material laws and affected by every wind that blows? Are we believing what the eyes report, what the ears hear, and what our culturally entrained habit of thought accepts? Or are we living in a perfect world, envisioning with the eyes of Spirit, listening with our inner ears attuned to Truth, functioning with a mind that is none other than the mind of God, the Source and Sustainer of all that is?

NO QUESTION, NO ARGUMENT; JUST CLEAR VISION

Truly, our world *is* our awareness of it. There is no question in us of how much wrongdoing there is in our world; the question is; instead, we ask: how much true belief have we accepted into our thought patterns?

We didn't come into this life to battle with dark ness — with thoughts or with weapons; our light effortlessly eliminates darkness. We don't make a barrier to keep out darkness; we simply bring the Presence that is our true Self to false beliefs.

It has been said, "Without a vision the people perish," and it is so. Without vision of the perfect universe, the heavenly Reality within, people do perish. This is so because ideas of outward things such as purported sickness, sin, danger, or death, lead to experiences of such things — and so the people perish by those things. This is the meaning of "the wages of sin (belief in absence of good, or separation from Source) are death."

Let us, therefore, bring our inner light into our world and let it shine. Let us see no separation, destruction, or opposition, but only Oneness, Unity, Omnipresence. This is repentance; this is the beginning of resurrection in each of us. And as we experience this resurrection, great glory shall illumine our whole universe and all our affairs.

In the New Testament we are told that Jesus lived this understanding. "I am the Light," he is reported as saying, referring to the light within all of us that will lighten any darkened sense. He understood that to be Self is to be Light, and continually turned his attention to the Light of his true Being, his eternal Self. This enabled him to transcend and transform experiences of this world, and led him to resurrection and ascension. And, in the apparent giving of his life, very publicly, in the crucifixion, he demonstrated the eternality of conscious ness — for himself and for all of us. Knowing that his Self could not die, he only experienced the appearance of death, dying to the dual-sighted eyes of material man.[18]

AN AGE OF AWAKENING

Today, we are experiencing a period of tremendous awakening. Where in past centuries only a very few of the people who were living in civilized, urbanized culture might have access to this knowledge, now anyone who can read or find a way to a teacher can learn these truths.[19]

---

[18] In alternative (Gnostic) versions of the gospels that were not included in the original bible during the Nicene Council in 325 C.E., there are stories of Jesus standing next to the grieving Peter during the crucifixion, saying "Why do you grieve? That's not me up there!" And in other versions, Jesus is said to have trained in India in several ashrams so that his spirit was able to enter and leave his body at will.

[19] DeWaters' original text was written in 1928-29, almost 100 years before this version. At that time, steamships were crossing the oceans in days, rather than months, airplanes were in use by the post office and military, radio and telegraph were normal, and telephones were becoming part of life. Newspapers, therefore, were able to provide information about people from the other side of the planet within hours or days, and men from India and China were teaching very publicly in Europe and America. How much more accurate is her description in this day of instant communication around the world, video recordings of

Progress and revelation such as has never been seen before in recorded history has appeared to human consciousness. This is the day of humanity's emancipation—delivery from the limitations of a dualistic materialist worldview and understanding. We are being freed from the limitations of time, of age, of disease, and all discord. Our new understandings and perceptions are dissolving past bonds and chains, through the power of our spiritual, irresistible, eternal Nature.

In this age of surprises, of visions and constant discovery, great illumination and inspiration are coming over individuals and groups, everywhere. Day by day, hour by hour, the heavenly possibilities come more clearly to the consciousness of humanity.[20]

It's happening in all areas of our lives. Music, for example, is expanding rapidly, and soon will be under stood to be fourth dimensional. No longer is it limited to the concert hall or home, but, through radio and recordings, is everywhere, available to all beings, uplifting them into a state of consciousness that transcends the circumstances of the moment. Often, too, people report hearing tones beyond those that were played and recorded. They seem to be hearing music emanating from another, larger world. Such melody is undimensional, unlimited, unconfined.

It's to be expected that in this emerging era of Insight, of spiritual Light, many wonderful things,

---

events being shared in the moment, and travel that takes only hours to go from one continent to another!

[20] DeWaters was writing at the time quantum theory was just emerging and Einstein's Theory of Relativity was first being published and tested. The ideas that there was something smaller than an atom, that matter and energy were interchangeable, and that time was relative, were surprising indeed!

unheard of in the past, shall be experienced around the world. In all areas of life — government, religion, ethnic divisions, and the social structures that support them — great changes are happening and will continue to do so, as humanity is lifted into this new state of being.

These changes are happening at this time because we are discovering Truth, and whenever we contact the true idea of a thing, the old, false idea falls away *automatically*. So, as we lift our vision to the Self-existent heights, we must certainly find the reality of vibrant health, pure joy, and irresistible glory entering our lives and radiating through all our experience.

TRUTH NOW

There is no limitation, no spot or blemish, upon any aspect of All That Is. The only limitation we experience is imposed by our false beliefs — and it is illusion, only. No evil is reported by those who are awakened. Neither the New Testament Jesus nor the Buddha beheld evil. Indeed, the Buddha offered a Way beyond all forms of distress, and Jesus is reported as having said that no evil will by any means hurt us. Jesus also said that anyone could handle serpents quite harmlessly, that even swallowing poison would not affect someone who was in the state of consciousness that the Buddha and the yogis call *samadhi*, that Jesus called "my name"[21] and his apostle, Paul, called "in the Spirit."

---

[21] The word "name" in English versions of the New Testament is one translation of the Aramaic and Hebrew word *shem* that must have been the original term used. The word *shem*, really means "character," "nature," "essence," "being," So when we say "in Jesus' name" or "in the name of Jesus Christ" we're saying that we are in that same state of consciousness, or nature, that Jesus lived in: the Christ mind.

Let us acknowledge these promises to be true *today*. Let us declare ourselves *now*, saying:

I am part of the One; I identify myself with the Source and Sustainer of Life.

I have absolute faith in the Truth of the unity of Being, of eternal Life.

I accept that the works done by Jesus and other spiritual avatars shall be done by me, through me, and in me, in this lifetime, because I now recognize that I am that same eternal Being, becoming ever more fully the One that Is, everywhere, always, NOW.

To perceive Unity, we must function from a state of consciousness above reason, above the relative mentality in which we were raised. We must; Truth is incomparable—beyond comparison! So, we do away with comparisons; we use our accepting mind, rather than our evaluating brain. One cannot measure how much greater Truth is than something else, or how much greater one belief is than another. We see that Truth always *is*. In this way, we experience Reality as our world of experience: "on earth as it is in heaven."

How can we expect to hold a vision of the being we've thought of as "without," if we're not considering the being within? How can we experience unity in the universe if we don't feel the unity of our own consciousness? So let us tell ourselves continually that the universe is within us, that what we see "out there" is reflecting, now, what we are experiencing within our own being.

How can we hope to see divine conditions around us if we haven't allowed them in our own being? How often have we failed to see the divine being at our door because we have not yet seen that divinity in our own hearts? For truly, it is the divine in you that is your power and glory.

It's easy to see a person as a prince when that per son is born in a palace, but what about the one born in a manger? It's easy to be brave and strong during times of peace, but how many of us can hold our own in the midst of apparent trials, tribulations and dangers?

Who, then, comes forth from the flaming furnace without even a trace of smoke in his clothing? Who feels the everlasting arms even while apparently falling into an abyss of darkness? Who sees dry land in the midst of the Red Sea? Only those with True vision; only those with Real faith; only those who know that the One is everywhere and always, as Love. That is, those who hold the vision of divine Life as all that is, both within and without.

So lift the veil from your eyes, as well as your inner vision, and behold the ONEness of life, the unity of be-ing, and let go of all ideas of separation, division, or comparison.

Recognizing that Truth is totality, we accept that Truth is the only substance that actually exists, now, throughout all that is — the substance that science calls the quantum field and is called *akasha* in Sanskrit. Even there, where the darkness appears, only light exists. Even in the gloomy glowering face we can behold the divinity that is so easy to see in the bright, smiling face of our beloved; we can say *Namaskar*.[22] Even where health is not visible to our eyes, our inner vision can be

---

[22] *Namaskar*, or in the more popular form, *Namaste*, is a Sanskrit term that means "the divinity in me beholds the divinity in you," and is a common form of greeting in India and other countries where Hinduism or Buddhism is a major religion.

hold the Health that is Truth and therefore must be present, here, now, and always.

∞

SUMMARY POINTS

- The belief that we are individual human beings, subject to errors of a material world, has resulted in all the limitation and discord present on Earth today.

- As Spirit is infinite and all, and Reality cannot be separated or divided, so we must be the Reality we have sought.

- The Christ/Krishna/Buddha essence of each of us says, "I am Life. I am Truth. I am the Source of all. I am God."

- These ancient teachers encouraged three steps to experience the Power of our true Self:

  1. Recognize that the world, the universe, is not a set of objects "out there," but is instead an image, a hologram, of our thoughts and vision.

  2. Recognize that any belief in distress of any kind, is the result of a lack of understanding and realization of the fullness, wholeness, completion, and unity of all that is.

  3. Fill our individual thoughts and feelings with, immerse our consciousness in, a full, clear vision of the heavenly Reality as ever present, recognizing all beings as immortal, perfect, and whole.

- The Book of Genesis mentions a second creation, an interpretation of the first; in which what was complete and whole is seen through worldly, materialist eyes — imperfectly and incompletely.

- Individual consciousness becomes aware of the original, perfect Creation by degrees, beholding more and more completely the perfection of the whole.

- Everywhere; day by day, hour by hour, Heaven is becoming clearer to the consciousness of humanity.

- Spiritual vision of oneself as free, flawless being blesses the mental plane of experience, and the brain begins to take on new thought patterns and new ideas of what is possible.

- Spiritual vision blesses our lives on the material plane, as well: the people around us act in more complete alignment with their true nature and the objects in our world take on a new beauty.

- It's not that Heaven is coming to us, or that Earth is coming to a heavenly state, but that "heaven is at hand," already present and all around us, ready for us to shift our conscious ness and allow ourselves to experience it,

- Since the world we experience is a reflection of our consciousness, then to judge any aspect of the world as not-good is to judge one's own thoughts and feelings as not-good.

- We didn't come into this life to battle with darkness with thoughts or with weapons; our inner light effortlessly dissolves darkness, wherever it may seem to be.

- Whatever we accept as reality, as power, as presence, constitutes our world at that moment.

- To perceive Reality, we function from a state of consciousness above reason, above the relative, evaluating mentality in which we were raised, and do away with comparisons.

- Recognizing that Truth is totality, we accept that Truth, in all its forms, must be the only substance that actually exists. Even where health is not visible to our eyes, our inner vision can behold the Health that is Truth and therefore must be present, here, now, and always.

- This is spiritual healing: any erring condition that one seems to experience is dissipated by our vision of the living Truth, which is our Christ/ Krishna/Buddha state of consciousness.

TO PONDER:

1. As you read the early chapters of Genesis in the Hebrew Bible or Christian Old Testament, in the second story, Adam is put to sleep, and never, in the whole Bible, does he wake up! Then all the people in the Bible are descended from him. What does this suggest to you about the nature of the world described by Bible based religions?

2. The Christ, the Buddha, Krishna, Lao Tse, and Rumi all offered a way of seeing the world that dissolves distress and encourages freedom through a transcendent vision of a Reality that is beyond the appearances of discord and

distress. How would you describe that way?

3. Consider someone who enters your awareness as unwell or unhappy. What is the Truth of that person? Can you see/hear/feel them as totally well in your inner vision? Can you allow that inner vision to become your outer experience? If not, what beliefs are preventing you from doing so?

4. What is your idea of a perfect Creation, a heavenly Reality? Can you allow yourself to experience elements of that Reality in your day-to-day life? If not, what beliefs are preventing you from doing so?

TO PRACTICE:

- For 3 days, tell yourself continually that the universe is within you, that what you see "out there" is reflecting what you are experiencing within your own being now.

- Each day, pay attention to how your experiences in the world and your thoughts and feelings align, and write down the ways they are unified.

Chapter Four

Practical Demonstrations

The great poets, mystics, saints, and reformers have all renounced personality, their egoic nature, in the favor of individuality, their divine Self. They are not swayed by opinions, nor moved by praise or censure. They look instead to the Light shining through their own souls.

We, like they, may possess any number of things — houses, land, friends, family — but we don't put our trust in them. Like the bird on a twig that sways beneath its light weight trusts its own wings instead of the twig, we look, not to the things around us, but to that deeper Wisdom within us, that greater Being that we are, to guide and sustain us from day to day.

Truth: Our Home

Truth is the health of our body. Truth is the breath of our life. Truth is the sparkle of our eyes, the laughter of our lips, the strength of our hands.

The robin's song is the One in each of us singing. The beauty of the flower is the One in us expressing. The charm of the evening and the breath of the morning — the pulse of all being — is the One that is the Truth of our being, expressing through us and around us.

We are like the "prodigal son" in the New Testament parable, who left his comfortable home to discover the world on his own terms, but spent all he had and discovered only disappointment and discomfort. Yet, one day he woke up and realized that his father's servants were living better than he now was. So he returned, thinking only to be hired as a servant — and was welcomed with great joy and feasting, as the long missed, much loved son of the household. Though he had been broken by his life experiences, nothing at his home was changed. Now he could live the life he was born to, in peace, comfort, and love.

So it is with all humanity, no matter how far one may have wandered in the dream appearances of life, no matter how far one may have fallen in belief, a welcome is ready for whoever wakes up and announces, "I will arise and go to my true Home."

Humanity too often forgets our first experience of the blaze of glory that we were born to. Too many of us lose sight of the spontaneous gladness which, like a sparkling stream, bubbles up from the living well within. Our innocence may be lost in the dream of the world, but our mature vision reminds us of the power that is born in us – power to part the Red Sea, to walk on water, to transform the ordinary into the extraordinary in any situation.

As we mature, books and teachers of Truth deliver a light to help us open our hearts and see the wonders of that Truth. They point us in the direction of the Home we are ready to return to. They help us learn to place our reliance on our own, radiant Self as the almighty Power, the changeless and imperishable Reality of our true world.

Remember, though, that it's the heart, not the head, that makes such wonders possible. Thought is not the way Home. Rather, as the famous monk, Brother Lawrence, learned, practicing the Presence[23] shows us that the Home we thought we left has always been right here, ready to welcome us back into the life

---

[23] *The Practice of the Presence of God*, Brother Lawrence (1620-1691).

we were born to live. Recognizing the Reality at hand, accepting the eternal Presence of the Christ/Krishna/ Buddha nature within us, speaking Truth as it is expressed through us, in all circumstances, is the way that takes us to our true Home.

When we shift our old sense of a separate personal state into the One impersonal God-state, we begin a new life. Laying down the untrue for the True, the limited for the Actual, the temporal for the Eternal, we find the "peace which passes understanding." We hear the Voice of Wisdom speaking in our soul, even as the disciples and apostles of the Buddha and the Christ heard it:

> I came to Earth to show you how to transcend the human state, the Earthbound state, and how to perceive and accept your perfect Spirit Self.
>
> All that you experience is Intelligence manifesting in ways that provide you with opportunities to see who you truly are. If these experiences did not provide contrast to your desired state, how would you come to use your power? If power is inert, dormant, unexpressed, what use is that power? If love were unknown, unfelt, how would you know its delight?
>
> Don't you remember the times you've been lifted high and received great illumination? When sickness was rolled back, and sorrow subsided like darkness before the light? These are the times when you were transformed with rapturous joy, unutterable peace, power, and glory. Then you have known Truth. Then you have felt Love. Then you have manifested that which you are: the One Self.

We've been taught that each of us is a human being born of human parents and that we are progressing through experience into health, wisdom, joy, and peace. Truth, however, proclaims (and is expressed in the teachings of the New Testament gospels, the *Bhagavad Gita*, the Buddhist Sutras, and Rumi's poems, among other sources), that we are inherently divine beings, *now*, and the road called progress and experience only discloses and reveals more of our perfection.

NOT EXTERNAL BUT INTERNAL

We learn, then, that the illumined path is not something to be found externally, but is rather something to be inwardly revealed. Our search for health and well-being, then, is not unlike a person's search for the glasses on their nose, or the phone in their hand.

It's like the person who starves even though their purse is full of gold. Seeking externally, studying and listening to others, taking medications, traveling and reading, too often takes one in a direction away from what is being sought.

In Truth, the seeker seeks that which all of us already are. The river of well-being already flows in and through each of us as everlasting Health. Our Buddha nature, Krishna driving the chariot of our life, the Christ Mind in each of us, says to us, "look within and find Me! ...The Power of Life, of Health, of Love is the essence of All that is, and it is to be found within! Focus on the inward divinity[24] to prosper and heal!"

Miracles are the measure of our acceptance of and reliance on the Power within each of us. "Cast your care upon me," says the inner Voice. And as we turn to that Voice, the radiance and quickening inspiration of the

---

[24] Although Buddhists generally do not "worship" a divine being, they do follow the Hindu tradition that *Brahman,* the Source and ground of being, individualizes in each person as *Atman,* called in this text, our spirit Self.

spirit Self instantly undoes and forgives any and all missteps and mistakes. This true Self places our being under the heavenly law of Love and wipes away any doubt that our fulfillment is at hand — immediately and in the moment. And it does so each time we turn to it!

DISPELLING DARKNESS

Lifting our inner vision to the Reality of the heavenly condition, we find the Light of Real Life entering our bodies and all our affairs. Our thoughts, refreshed and restored, are filled with joyous songs of glory. We delight in this world that has become our true Home, returned from the wanderings of the dream we had been living. We are with our Source, and no longer concern ourselves with the state of the body or other appearances — all of which have been based on falsehoods up to now.

A falsehood, of course, has no substance. As there is nothing to sustain it, it must disintegrate in the presence of Truth, just as darkness is dissolved in the presence of light. A story is told that exemplifies this experience.

A group of people living in a cave in the high mountains of the Himalayan range had never experienced fire. They heated their food in the light of the sun and led their lives according to the presence or absence of the sun's warming rays.

Over time, they began be overcrowded and wished they could see what was in the depths of their cave, and maybe use that space, as well, but they were afraid. For years they had told each other stories of the evil beings and great monsters who lived in the darkness beyond their safe home, and some were sure they'd even seen them.

Some among them decided that maybe the evil in the darkness would leave if they prayed to it, and they did, but still the darkness remained, unyielding. Then someone suggested they could fight it—that they should take their hammers and clubs and beat it into submission as they did with the beasts they hunted, but that, it seemed was impossible; the darkness was unaffected by their violence toward it Some thought that if they fasted and sacrificed, the darkness would go away, but that didn't work either.

Finally, a man from the world beyond discovered them. He stayed with them a few days and heard their tales of the evil darkness that lingered in the depths of the cave and how they had tried to dispel it.

The man listened and told them that the only way to dispel darkness was light. He then proceeded to gather sticks and create torches. Then he built a small fire— the first they had seen—and lit the torches.

The people were in awe! The sun had been brought down from the sky into their cave!

Then the man gave each of the bravest cave dwellers a torch to carry—what a wonder! Fearful, yet hopeful, they followed the man into the depths of the cave, far beyond anywhere any of their people had ever gone.

Deeper and deeper they went, finding only rock and sand along the way. No monsters. No evil beings. Not even any great darkness!

In the light of their torches, the darkness was absent. Their wish was granted: the darkness that had haunted them for generations was dispelled, never to haunt them again.

And so it is for each of us. Whenever we accept the Light of Truth, some of the darkness that has haunted us is dispelled, never to haunt us again. And as we go deeper and deeper into the darkness that we believed was there, it, too, is dissolved in the Light that we carry — and are.

THE HEAVENLY REALITY

This is how it is for anyone who has glimpsed the heavenly Reality, our true Home; the world of space, time, and material objects is never again quite so real. Those who pass above the plane of thought and matter, looking out and beyond into the Perfect Land, are filled with a new ecstasy and joy, beyond any ever experienced in this life before.

In this land of glory there is no separation of people, things, or ideas. It's a universe of Truth and Love, of joyous Splendor and ever-increasing Glory. Here one is un bounded, unlimited, free as air.[25] Here beautiful thoughts come bubbling up from within like sparkling waters and become manifest immediately in Love and Light.

No suggestion of sin, fear, sickness, or destruction is even considered on this plane of existence, for this is the Reality of perfect Light; the Reality of ideal Harmony. This is the heavenly Reality, the place of the loving and beloved Heart.

A LIVING LANGUAGE

Once we've experienced inspiration lighting the fire within and removing the darkness, we feel a great expansion: a freedom and independence not known before. We find our statements of Truth, our spiritual affirmations, becoming more and more alive, filled with a new kind of power. No longer do our affirming sentences seem mere words, like so many sounds or letters of the alphabet strung together. Now they take on fresh

---

[25] This description matches the descriptions of people who have had Near Death Experiences – their heart and brained have flatlined for a time, and they have felt themselves being drawn to their spiritual Home.

meaning, sometimes seeming to glow on the page; occasionally even seeming like living beings.

Soon, after having caught glimpses of the finished Reality, a new language is spoken. Many words reveal a new meaning. For example, the word health used to be associated with only the body, but now Health is seen to be universal, omnipotent, and omnipresent. Like sun shine and the fact that 2+2=4, Health is now understood to be a fact of being, Omnipresent.

Then other words join with Health: Freedom, Life, Love, Grace, Peace, Power, and more. We feel their universal quality and substance, and we realize that the perfect universe that they describe is at hand. We behold it in us and the world around us, as did Jesus the Christ, Gautama the Buddha, Rumi the Sufi poet, and Lao Tse the ancient Chinese master.

At this point, each of these qualities is recognized in everything, though attached to nothing; is seen as the Reality of our lives. Now the Spirit within and around us is one perfect, ideal Being: in us, as us, and working through us for us and for all beings.

Spirit is the fact that there is no limit of health for the body, no limit of wisdom in the mind. Spirit is the fact that there is no stopping place for Life, no boundary to Health, no termination for Joy, Peace, or Delight. Spirit is the experience that "the desert shall rejoice and blossom as the rose... the eyes of the blind shall be opened, and the ears of the deaf shall be unstopped... the lame shall leap... and the tongues of the dumb shall sing."[26]

---

[26] This is the prophecy in the Old Testament/Hebrew Bible book of Isaiah that is usually spoken at Christmas time, and is the chorus of the song "Mary Did You Know?"

UNLIMITED BEINGS

We are living *now,* and Spirit is the fact that this life will never cease, for even one instant, to be. Spirit is why we are beings of intelligence, power, and glory without end, and why we are divine, eternal, irresistible Self: Truth.

As Spirit we drink the water of Life freely, and the path of illumination shines before us, bright with living glory. Because we are Spirit, the One Presence is known, felt, and understood; the age of boundless freedom, love, glory, and indescribable splendor is observed here and now.

Our Spirit-Self, our God-being, is not subject to material law any more than a flying bird is subject to the laws governing plants rooted in the ground. With the fire of insight, *we know and insist that we are immune to any sense of limitation, bondage, or distressing circumstances.* Therefore, as Spirit beings, we recognize, affirm, and declare that we are not subject to the laws of matter, because *we are free in heavenly Reality.* As Jesus declared, these things (the results of materialist beliefs) shall not harm us, because there is no harm in unreality.

APPEARANCES ARE NOT REALITY

The instant we replace untrue thoughts (called "darkness") with ideas based on spiritual principles ("light"), the out-picturing changes, and all appearances of distress or disease ("darkness") are dissolved in the light of changeless Reality.

The conditions pictured in the body called disease are not at all what they seem to those with unenlightened vision. The report of the senses is that the disease is in or on the body, that the trouble is external. But this is a totally erroneous idea, for what is seen in the body that we call disease is a *picture only* and is no more in the body than a horse pictured on the motion picture screen is actually standing on the screen.

With all that in mind, let's consider what ideas are truly based on the principles of spiritual science.

- One of the first is that our spiritual source and supply, a single spiritual being, called Spirit or God, is omnipresent, everywhere present, not absent in any part of the infinite universe or our lives.

- Following on that principle is the realization that, if all that exists is that one Spirit, or God, and if any person exists, then every person — including myself — must be Spirit, God, as well.

- Another principle is that Spirit is not subject to any belief not in harmony with the good of the whole — or any part of the whole; no belief in distress or disease touches the Universal Spirit, or affects it in any way.

- The understanding that we are Spirit, and that Spirit is not subject to any belief not in harmony with the good of the whole, leads us to the realization that, as no false idea exists in the Christ/ Krishna/Buddha mind within each of us, so no false or disharmonious idea can exist in our mind; the "darkness" of disharmony/disease/ distress is dispelled.

- *Truth being what we are, nothing can be against us.* Realizing that no disharmony is possible, we stop fearing it.

Filling our thoughts and feelings with these truths, and with words describing the qualities of Spirit (Peace, Love, Joy, Harmony, etc.), our vision becomes aligned with Spirit.

We see Spirit creating in, through, as, and around us, and so we ask "How could anything ever hinder us from experiencing and expressing the omnipotence that we *are*? And we realize the one Truth: *there is no thing and no way that can keep us from the wonderful bliss and glory that is our true nature*; it is already present in our being.

We fill our minds with this idea, letting all our thoughts and words reflect on it, until the Truth of it becomes fully alive in us — the only possible experience, the only out-picturing, in our lives. We are then identified, unified, with Spirit, the Source, Presence, Power, and supply that works in and through All That Is for the good of all.

ONE PERFECT BEINGNESS

Then no more questions are needed; no doubt remains. Only almighty Truth exists, in us and around us, expressing and experiencing more and more beauty, joy, love, and all the other qualities that we have called divine.

Accepting that we are Spirit, our vision is clear and constant; we cannot lose our vision of eternal, changeless, harmonious existence. Accepting the Real Truth of our being, our thoughts and ideas are pure and complete, and our bodies and world, manifesting our beliefs, are free of all possibilities of distress or disease — of any imperfection, whatever.

When we watch a video, the images and characters seem to be alive, but nothing is actually happening on that screen. Nothing is being moved or changed. Similarly in life: nothing is being healed or removed or changed by our actions. Our experience of the world follows our mental activity, just as the image on the screen follows the programming in the electronics.

We correct the programming of our brains and the images of darkness are dissolved. It's not that we've created health and harmony on the screens of our bodies; they have always been there waiting for us to tune into them. We have eliminated the block in our thinking, changed the tuning on the receiver that is our brain, and accepted that which was always at hand.

Then, once we realize that *all* images of darkness and limitation are a function of the programming of our brains, and not the Reality of us, we rise to a new level of being; we are born anew.

Our new life, free from the limitations of the old beliefs and resulting appearances, shouts with joy, "Oh, Freedom!" "Free at last!" "No more bondage or limitations — only Freedom in the Power of the One That Is!" "All Glory to the Power Within!"

The living Truth sweeps over our universe, making itself known, seen, and felt — hour by hour and minute by minute — ushering in a new, Golden Age of boundless freedom, irresistible love, indescribable splendor, and transcendent glory.

BODY AS BEING IN FORM

Let us acknowledge that the body is the means through which the Being that we are, our Spirit-Self, brings itself into expression and action. The body is imperturbable, indestructible, everlasting, eternal Being: Infinite Life in individual form: *Being and body are one.*

Let all sense of division and separation depart from your thought. We are not trying to unite God and man, soul and body. Our clear vision reports that God and man, soul and body, Spirit and form, Cause and effect,

Infinite Life and its individual expression, are one *now, always, and forever.*

Being newborn in Spirit, fulfilling the biblical injunction that the body is transformed by the renewing baptism of Spirit, we gently and without effort transcend all experiences that aren't harmonious with body, mind, and spirit. With Jesus, Krishna, and the Hindu saint Mahababaji,[27] we accept our inherent immortality. Mind, imbued with spiritual understanding dispels any illusions and dissolves any erroneous beliefs.

A PROCESS

Progress is the process by which, in stages of development through states of consciousness, our human senses become aware of our spiritual nature and reaches the point of ascension—beyond all beliefs of mortal being and material universe. And we are progressing.

In each and every hour, this lovely planet Earth is taking on more and more of the Heavenly glory as we press forward. People are waking up and deserts are becoming fertile. In cities and villages around the world, humanity is uniting in thought, awareness, and action, in a new kind of peaceful power that can lead only to harmonious wellbeing for all. The seventh angel, of fulfillment and rest, approaches.

Let us acknowledge that the time is come, the hour is here. The angel of Insight gently whispers, "be of good

---

[27] In the Kriya Yoga tradition, brought to the U.S. by Paramahansa Yogananda, a man who was born in the 1400s currently lives in the Himalayas, meditating with his disciples, and appearing occasionally in peoples' lives, as a youth, about 18 years old. He is said to be the teacher of Yogananda's teacher.

cheer" to all who will listen, all over this beautiful, supporting planet.

As more and more people hear it, as Spirit is accepted to be the life of all, when we are certain that we all have the same Life, the same Being, the same Reality, then the divine body appears in us and as us. Spirit is not regenerated; humanity is regenerated.

Three Stages

The dematerialization of our body and spiritualization of our thoughts is one process. Through vision and practical demonstration, our sense of mortality seems to pass through three stages before yielding completely to the Truth of our immortality. They are: atonement, resurrection, and ascension.

1. At-One-Ment. We call the dawning upon human awareness of our sinless, perfect state, atonement, or, more accurately, atonement. It's the understanding that, as "Light shines in darkness," it's impossible for what we call evil (all destruction, disease, and death) to have any power or even existence. We realize that, because the world around us reflects our own consciousness, there can therefore be no external evil. The good is always shining in our consciousness, but when the good is obscured by misperceptions, then the result has been called "bad" or "evil." As a result, whatever is called evil is like a cloud that seems to block the light even though the sun's light shines constantly, regardless. At-one-ment (atonement), therefore, is the realization of one Presence as *always* present, everywhere, in all situations; that all that changes is one's belief about it. It's the

realization that all forms of distress, all that's been called bad or evil, are the result of misperceptions — the result of not clearly perceiving the Presence, the Light, that is always there.

2. Resurrection. We call the practical demonstration of atonement, resurrection, which is a restoration — the restoring to our aware ness our innate power and glory, our original dominion over the forms of matter. It's the restoring of something that was never lost or lacking, except in our beliefs. The experience of resurrection is, therefore, the practice of Truth-full vision and ideas. As higher and higher concepts of health and immortality are realized, naturally one embodies and expresses them. Resurrection, therefore, is self-improvement, self-purification, and awakening from a dream of duality and opposites to the perception and acceptance of oneness that has been called "practicing the Presence."

3. Ascension. Letting go of the total renunciation of any idea of mortality, then, is Ascension. It's the conscious experience of our eternal identity, the Truth of our being. It's the return of the Prodigal Child[28] within each of us to our Home, our infinite, eternal, being, in unconditional love.

---

[28] This, as all uses of the term "Prodigal" in this book, is a reference to the parable in the New Testament gospels, of the boy who left home, having been given his share of the inheritance he would have otherwise received at the end of his father's life, spent it all in the ways that young people do, and ended up working feeding pigs. He realizes that his father treats servants better than he is being treated so he goes home to ask for a job. The father is overjoyed to see his son return, calls for a big celebration, and reinstates him in the family.

Having taken the steps of atonement, accepting a Truth-full perception of reality, then gone on to the steps of resurrection (practice of the One as Present in All), the Prodigal within each of us finally loses all sense of mortality and gains awareness of our spiritual preexistence and continuing life. We now enter spiritual rest and find eternal peace *while still in our bodies.*

A HIGHER LIFE

As we learn this Science of the Absolute, we enlarge our own capacity and begin to live a higher life. As our material perceptions — those reporting pain, limitation, discord — are understood as *false*, and our deeper, spiritual knowing — of joy, health, and harmony — is recognized as the always-present *Reality,* we begin to use our infinite power to establish a perfectly harmonious daily life.

We accept and embody Truth. We individualize the Power that is our Source and demonstrate, to our own satisfaction, the falsity of limitation and of bondage. As a result, the doors of our hearts, and any form of prison, are opened and we, the captives within them, are set free.

Because spiritual ideas deliver us from the physical perception, we are led to divine heights, and our material sense of existence is exchanged for our Spirit existence. *As consciousness is lifted, untrue beliefs and ideas are gently left behind*, and each of us demonstrates our true authority over all sense experiences, including sin, sickness, and discord of any kind.[29] Rising to our

---

[29] There is a tradition that Gautama Buddha, as he was wandering with his monks, was approached by an angry townsman who berated him for

new, truer sense of Self, we dwell in infinite harmony — complete, perfect, immutable, and incorruptible.

THE POWER OF TRUTH

This is not a method of mind over matter, nor even mind over mind. Instead, it is the divine process of spiritualizing thought and sense, demonstrating the omnipotence of the Truth of our being over the false beliefs learned in the past, and choosing the real, Spiritual essence over false, material perceptions.

Truth, gloriously omnipotent, is supreme. Awareness of this fact redeems us from fear, renews faith, and lifts our affections to a new level.

As we gain the vision of ourselves as eternal Life, irresistible Truth, and exalting Love, we lose all fear and boldly live from our new Understanding.

Accepting our true heritage, our reality as the Spirit-Self, the Christ/Krishna/Buddha nature, that we have discovered within, we don't hesitate to stand forth in our knowledge of the presence of our Spirit-Source within, the new basis of our faith.

THE ULTIMATE ATTAINMENT

What higher attainment could we achieve than Ascension? What can melt away any sense of fear and darkness except the understanding of our Spirit-Self, our True Being? Only false beliefs conceal the Reality of our beingness from our experience. As we overcome all ideas of sin, sickness, distress of any kind, we are

---

all the ways he was undermining the cultural norms and turning young men away from family traditions, calling him all sorts of names. The Buddha took it all silently and then said "Thank you. That was the last one."

led to an even greater glory, the overcoming of death. Nothing but such spiritualization of thought and vision can open the gates of Paradise that are always present, above and beyond material perception.

Spiritual understanding is the Light that places our feet on the firm ground of Heaven on Earth, establishing its own principle in our thought patterns by demonstrations of Truth in our lives.

This Truth, this reality of all-inclusive Good, never disappeared from our spiritual sight, but remains forever intact, omnipresent and fully tangible to our immortal consciousness. This reality of eternal, continuous harmony is here, now, awaiting our individual recognition and acceptance.

The great Islamic poet, Rumi, tells us,

How wonderful, how wonderful is the Reality of Love!
O Love's face which is more Soul than soul!
O Reality of Love which is better than any position, even better than soul!
I have been freed from worshipping, from ostentation.
I understand that their source is the Reality of Love.

This reality, therefore, which is within us as our true Self, is our Real Home. It was always here, is here now, and always will be ours to choose.

To the extent that our consciousness aligns with and, ultimately becomes, the One, divine Source, the perfection and completeness of this reality becomes our experience. To the extent that we recognize this Self, which we truly are, as The Way, and as we align and accept this Self *as* who we are, we can say, with the Christ/Krishna/Buddha, "I am the Way."

DEMONSTRATION

Those instructed in this Science of the Absolute have grasped this glorious view of their own Self as all-knowing, all-mighty, all-inclusive. Practicing this understanding, they then ascend the scale of being and emerge gently into a new Life, everlasting. As we are awakened to the perception of who we are, one with the Source and Sustainer of all that is, we are lifted to a higher plane of experience, and so it becomes effortless to demonstrate health and harmony in every aspect of our lives.

Truth leads the eager and ready heart onward and upward, advancing us spiritually and disclosing the ultimate realization of the Reality of everlasting harmony and glory *within our own power and demonstration.* And, as the reality of the Reality within us is brought to light, our awareness is lifted, and the spiritual idea of Life is revealed as always working and practical.

Then, immersed in our own divine illumination and spiritual awareness, we can assert our mastery, our total control, over any appearance of disease, fear, or bondage around us. We prove without doubt that divine Understanding, Intelligence, Wisdom is omnipotent — the only power in all situations.

Practical demonstration, then, is the act of Truth dissolving material beliefs and uplifting faith and vision to discern perfect Creation, permanent, changeless, untouched by any human ideas, here, now.

Through our spiritual understanding and identification with our own spirit-Self, we easily dissolve old thoughts that were based on external perceptions and training. Now we can stand firm and unfaltering, realizing that nothing can deprive us of our complete demonstration of health, harmony, and happiness.

All there is to the ideas of sin, sickness, and death is a false claim, and no false idea can affect the power of our own true Self or deprive anyone of a continuous sense of life and immortality. The fact of perfect being is the only Truth, the one, ideal vision to hold on to: perfect Being, perfect ideas, perfect expression.

Focusing our thoughts on the ideal vision, we master the false idea of material laws, and end their limitations on our experience. Applying this practice to human experience lifts individual consciousness above their old perceptions, removing fear and false belief and revealing the all-power and ever-presence of spiritual Law and Presence that is the Reality abiding within each of us.

Thus, through this Absolute Science, each of us may lift our consciousness higher, to another level of being, in which it's possible to identify our own selves with the Christ/Krishna/Buddha nature and so experience total freedom, victorious over false ideas, triumphant over false appearances. This is Ascension.

SUMMARY POINTS
- In this Science we look not to the things around us, but to that deeper Wisdom within us, that greater Being that we are, to guide and sustain us from day to day.
- Humanity is like the "prodigal son" in the New Testament parable, who left his comfortable home to discover the world on his own terms but spent all he had and discovered only

disappointment and discomfort, then woke up and realized his father's servants were living better than he, so returned to be hired as a servant—and was welcomed with great joy and feasting, and restored to his honored place in his father's home.

* Our innocence may be lost in the dream of the world, but our mature vision reminds us of our true Home, and of the power that is born in us—power to part the Red Sea, to walk on water, to transform the ordinary into the extraordinary in any situation.

* Thought is not the way Home; it is the heart, not the head, that makes such wonders possible.

* For anyone who has glimpsed the heavenly Reality, which is our true Home, the world of space, time, and material objects is never again quite so real, and some of the darkness that has haunted us is dispelled, never to haunt us again.

* No suggestion of sin, fear, sickness, or destruction is even considered on this plane of existence; this is the reality of perfect Light, the reality of ideal Harmony.

* Spirit is the fact that there is no limit of health for the body, no limit of wisdom in the mind, no end for Life, no boundary to Health, no termination for Joy, Peace, or Delight.

* These qualities are recognized in everything, though attached to nothing, and seen as the Reality of our lives: one perfect, ideal Being, in us, as us, and working through us for us and for all beings, to experience them more fully.

- Being Spirit, we are immune to any sense of limitation, bondage, or evil; we are free in heavenly Reality.
- Ascension is having let go of any idea of mortality and limitation, the conscious experience of our eternal identity, the return of the Prodigal Child within each of us to our Home, experiencing Truth in unconditional love.
- Practical demonstration is our knowledge of Truth dissolving material beliefs and uplifting faith and vision to discern the perfect Creation — permanent, changeless, untouched by any human ideas — here, now, as our only experience.

TO PONDER:

1. Does the idea of unlimited power excite or frighten you? Think about all the stories and statements you've heard about power — what it is, what it does to the people who have it, what kind of people have it or want it, what using it means, how it shows up in the natural world — and write them down. Look over your list and cross off each negative statement and write a positive one to replace it — if that seems difficult, reason out how the negative statement is part of a culture that is built on the idea of controlling the population for the benefit of a few, and how it would be different in an earth-centered, egalitarian culture.

2. Consider your life as a novel or a movie. How would you rewrite the script? You can start as early as your conception, all the way to this

moment now, and forward. Consider yourself as an actor playing the role that has your name, and the other people in your life as characters in this story, played by other actors whom you've al- ways admired and appreciated. Consider the world around you as a movie set that can be changed to fit the unfolding script. How does that change your feelings about your life history? About your present circumstances?

3. If you knew that the whole universe is designed in a way that you, and everyone around you, may fulfill your deepest longings here and now, what would you be doing? Thinking? Saying? Feeling?

TO PRACTICE:

- Apply your current understanding of practical demonstration by using Truth to dissolve your material beliefs about some experience and uplifting your faith and vision to discern perfect Creation, permanent, changeless, untouched by any human ideas, here, now.

- Write down your process: what did you think was happening? What aspect of Truth did you replace the idea behind that experience with? When and where did this happen? When did you see the appearance based on old ideas and training dissolve into the Reality of heavenly life?

Chapter 5

Accurate Interpretations

When someone brings us information that doesn't seem true to us and we choose to determine if it is accurate, we begin to trace that statement back to its origin. We unravel the story, bit by bit, until we are satisfied that we have established its accuracy.

It's easier to determine whether something is true when we've had the experience of something that is genuine and real. If we've been raised in an environment of lies and untruths, we are less able to recognize what the actual truth of a situation is: what is harmonious with universal processes, what resonates with our hearts. Then, once we've experienced the "genuine article" — whether it be a child's unconditional love for us, or a sincere compliment from a friend, or the working out of a complex reasoning process, or a mystical experience of the oneness of all that is — we feel compelled to find it everywhere, to penetrate the lies and expose the truth itself, once more.

Having grown up in a world of lies and falsehoods, we look at life through a veil, see everything inverted, so Truth seems impossible. But stripping off the veil of illusions[30] we can penetrate the mist and begin to perceive Truth as all Reality, and to recognize that the unreality we were taught to focus on is actually nothing.

---

[30] DeWaters is using a bit of a pun here: the "veil of illusion" is also a reference to the "veil of the temple" that was "rent from the top down" at the moment of Jesus' death on the cross, according to the New Testament. That veil was a curtain that was hung in front of the "holy of holies," the innermost chamber where the Ark of the Covenant—and hence, God, was located.

So now, whenever Truth is expressed or Reality is our experience, we recognize it immediately. Our body and soul respond in a special way, which may at first feel strange, but soon becomes a welcome experience that we look forward to happening again, soon.[31]

And whenever we encounter the unreality or false hood brought about by past beliefs, we do not attend to the report itself, nor even the condition or situation. Instead, we use our spiritual vision to look *beyond* the false testimony and material form to perceive the Truth that is standing in its place, Truth that has seemed concealed from view by the veil of illusion.

LIGHT BEYOND THE DARKNESS

In the book of John in the Christian New Testament, it is written, "The light shines in darkness, and the darkness does not comprehend it."

If we perceive the light that is shining, the darkness that didn't comprehend it is dissolved. In other gospels Jesus is reported as saying "*You* are the light... the Kingdom is within *you*." Looking toward this light, this Reality of our being, it becomes clear that any condition that isn't filled with that Light, that Life, is unreal. Instead, it is a falsity based on an untrue belief in darkness.

At the same time, we recognize that back of that false belief is a *Reality of perfect, changeless being,* and back of any untrue expression of inharmony or discord shines this Reality: *perfect, changeless, and immortal*

---

[31] For some, the experience of Truth is felt in the body as "goose bumps"—also called "God bumps" or "spirit sparkles." Emma Curtis Hopkins called it the "deep thrill of cool fire." For others, it is a sense of relaxation of tension, or of "fit." Still others become aware of a deep stillness and satisfaction.

embodiment. We do not let a sense of sympathy go toward the individual who claims to be experiencing falsely, nor to the condition that person states is the reason for their false belief. Instead, we realize that the onlooker is seeing an unreality, rather than seeing the universe truly. For if anyone sees the universe as the heavenly structure it truly is, there would be no occasion for sympathy, fear, or disturbance.

As we see all forms in alignment with our spiritual insight or Vision, we see the changeless, perfect, immaculate being that they truly are; we are mindful only of Reality. We see that, just as the identity of what is first perceived as a crawling caterpillar and later as a beautiful, soaring butterfly, never changes, so the individual identity of all beings is Self and is therefore constant, un changeable, and immortal, no matter what form any on looker may perceive, believe, or claim. As Krishna tells us in the Hindu *Bhagavad Gita*, "The embodied soul is eternal in existence, indestructible, and infinite, only the material body is factually perishable," and later, "There was never a time when you and I and all those gathered here have not existed; nor will there be a time when we will cease to exist."

Once we've grasped this fact, we begin immediately to interpret all our experience according to this delightful Reality. As we recognize and accept that our individual identity is forever established, perfect, and complete, without beginning or end, we realize that any untrue experience is based in physical perception, supported by culturally conditioned ideas of discord, disease, or disturbance. These ideas and experiences are contrary to the principle of changeless identity and therefore cannot be accepted as having the slightest vestige of Truth. So, regardless of the intensity of the appearance, no matter what depth of darkness seems not to comprehend the light in a situation, the fact in every case is that *perfect being and perfect universe are now at hand for us to behold and experience.*

Let it be clearly understood that any being who seems at one time mortal and another time immortal *is one entity.* Although it can be said that a caterpillar is not a butterfly, yet we know that when we see one, we see both: *they are the same identity.*

So it is with a human being. Any of us may be seen, through physical perception, as mortal, limited form, while with spiritual vision and insight we behold the perfect, divine Being. Regardless, each of us actually is one constant, uninterrupted, eternal expression of the One.

This is why we need not sympathize with someone who is apparently shadowing forth some untrue experience. Instead of sympathizing with a mistaken interpretation, we bring the light of Truth to the consciousness of that person. We dissolve the darkness with Light.

TRUE VISION IN PLACE OF ERRING BELIEF

When one is believing in something that is untrue, believing some false condition to be present which actually is not, metaphysicians call this "false belief." It is this false belief that must be met and overcome, and we do so with Truth, the right idea, the accurate interpretation.

What causes darkness to disappear from a room is light, and what causes false belief to disappear from one's thoughts is true belief. Belief in Truth is what metaphysicians call "true belief," or right interpretation of experience. As we exercise this right interpretation of experience, we find the kingdom of Heaven in our consciousness — and world.

This is because a true belief has very real substance and power supporting it: the Substance and Power of Spirit. The underlying basis of any true belief (say, the belief in one continuous identity of being) must be the absolute Truth, the Source itself.

By contrast, an untrue belief has nothing supporting it whatsoever. Only someone else's words, or our own misunderstanding of an early experience are the basis for any belief in limitation, lack, or distressing outcomes. Such beliefs are nothing but a misinterpretation of that which is actually present, Spirit in form, which can only be perfect and true.

Therefore, one does not treat disease, sorrow, or any disorder as though it were actual, but instead we see that this is the out-picturing of some false belief held in the neural networks of the brain, and that, as soon as the true belief is accepted, its Truth will be the Light that illuminates the universe for all involved, transforming the experience into Heaven.

Holding to the realization that we are Life, we are Truth, we are Spirit, we feel firmly supported in Real Substance and the flow of omnipotent Reality within us. With our eyes clear and our feet firmly planted on that which truly is, the untrue experience vanishes and utterly disappears.

Not that any real change has taken place — to think so is not clear understanding. It's simply that now one has a fuller awareness of the Reality that is here, now, and so experiences a more accurate interpretation of the conditions of the moment: one experiences the heaven that is always at hand instead of the appearance built up by false beliefs.

We transcend beyond any experience of distress, disease, or disturbance as we accept the true belief. "The happiness which ... leads to the end of suffering... arises from the serenity of one's own mind," says Krishna in the *Bhagavad Gita*, and also Gautama Buddha in his *Sutras*. "Nothing shall in any way hurt you," is the promise of Jesus in the New Testament.

Nothing external is to be changed, healed, or removed. As we fully comprehend this, we achieve the clear Vision that is Ascension. Rather than going outward to conquer darkness or distress, we go *inward* only, where we find the Truth: that we *are* Omniscience, Omnipresence, Omnipotence. In this realization we find the interpretation of all experience that uplifts all humanity; we find the Krishna/Buddha/Christ within.

Like children who suddenly comprehend the fact that "2 and 2 are 4", which they have known all along without realizing it, we begin to comprehend what we already know: our own immortality. And, just as those children all come to that understanding, we all must someday come to the realization of the Truth that is already within us: our freedom from the limitations of matter, our own divine nature.

In some ways, our situation is like the old parable of the lion cub who, being raised by sheep, thought and acted like a sheep — until he encountered a mature lion and realized who and what he really was. Similarly, raised and taught by beings who believed themselves to be mortal, we have thought and acted like mortal beings, not realizing who and what we truly are.

The Hebrew prophet Isaiah is reported in the Jewish Bible (the Christian Old Testament) as having described the coming messiah as "almighty God, the everlasting Father" incarnate. Jesus, described in the Christian New Testament as having fulfilled all the prophecies, saw the perfect Kingdom and stated that "all may be one." He stands before us as a model of what we actually are, telling us in *The Course in Miracles*, that he is an elder brother, one who can show us the path because he has taken it before us.

In that marvelous parable told above, the lion cub who thought he was a sheep gazed upon the full-grown lion silhouetted on the hillside, enraptured, and the old, limited idea of himself as a sheep simply fell away; he woke up to his true nature. So we too, as we gaze upon the ideal being, Jesus, called the "lion of Judah," find our old, limited ideas of who and what we are dissolving, to be replaced by Truth: our real, immortal, perfection and power.

In a world where people all around believed they were limited human beings and experienced sickness, sin, and death as their beliefs led them, Jesus came one day and stood before them, a glorious being of transcending majesty. And, gazing upon this ideal, many felt something give way within them — their human beliefs in fear, control, and limitation vanished. Recognizing God in human form, they accepted the possibility of such a state for themselves, and they took on their rightful heritage: the kingdom of perfection.

And still, today, this Ideal Presence is here, standing before us, saying "Lo, I am with you always... I will never leave you nor forsake you." We find guideposts and pointers in the scriptures: the New Testament, the

Buddhist *Sutras*, and the *Bhagavad Gita*, but we find the actual Presence within our own hearts.

And, gazing upon this Ideal, this Christ/Krishna/ Buddha nature, within and around us, we too have felt something give way within us. We realize the meaning lessness and emptiness of the limiting beliefs that we're "only human."

As we continue to gaze upon the Ideal, the Christ/ Krishna/Buddha being that has been glowing on the mountain top of possibility, we begin to feel it also within us, and we accept it as our own true Identity. And, as this liberating process unfolds, we begin to accept our own, true power over all that is material. Rapturously, spontaneously, we find ourselves becoming the very Power and Presence that we've been seeking. We see the deliverance that we are. We behold the heavenly realm that is our Home. We take on our God-being. All Hail!

Then, taking on our true Identity, we enter the paradise that is prepared for us — both in the beginning, as described in the Hebrew book of Genesis, and in the end, as described in the Christian book of Revelation. And as we enter, we find infinite Peace and a Joy that is beyond expression.

BEYOND TIME, PLACE, PERSONALITY

Applying this sublime vision to the many seeming problems of everyday experience, we find that we can experience instant joy, satisfaction, and freedom by realizing a truer interpretation of time, place, and personality.

Time, for example, often seems to hinder our experience of joy. There's sometimes a sense that it will be next week or next year before our good is disclosed, rather than NOW, today; that great abundance is somewhere in the future rather than here, at hand.

To the spiritual eye, however, there is no division, no separation whatever: in space or in time. Does our God-Self establish a difference in conditions between last year and today? Between a year from now and today? No. Whatever is true is *always* true. As the apostle Peter said in a letter to the early Christians: "One day is with the Lord as a thousand years, and a thousand years as one day." And those who have been clinically dead and returned to tell about the experience consistently say that there is no sense of time "on the other side." So, *if it is ever true that I have abundance of all good, then it must be true now and for all time.*

An experience with a student brought this home. A telephone message from one of the author's[32] students was asking for help. She stated that she did not know which way to turn for supply, that her demonstration always seemed to depend on some future event that never happened, or on certain people who didn't fulfill her expectations. Putting down the phone the above quote from Peter immediately came to mind. It was radiantly clear that if the student would be helped next week or next year, she had received this help a thousand years ago. Eternity is here and at hand: "the same yesterday, today, and forever," and what is called a division of time, such as a day, a month, a year, is merely a material interpretation of the changeless Reality. Only in the material world do we have time; in the transcendent Heavenly world, we have *eternity.*

---

[32] DeWaters, a Christian Science practitioner who found the teachings limited, went off on her own (as did Joel Goldsmith), is relating a personal experience here.

Distance, also must be nonexistent in the Heavenly Reality, and realizing that the student mentioned relying on people at a distance from her, the author saw that distance, like time, is a false sense arising from a belief in separation, and this false sense could have no real effect at all. Infinity cannot be divided or separated. Infinite presence is One Presence. Whatever abundance is "there" must be, in infinity, also "here," always (eternity) everywhere (infinity).

Personality, too, becomes nothing in the awareness of the One Being that is All That Is. The author accepted the nothingness of individual personality and realized that demonstration depends solely on one's sacred Spirit-Self, *always, everywhere, one Being.* Joyfully basking in this wonderful awareness of never-beginning, never-ending Eternity and Being, the author knew, and could feel, that the student who asked for help was also aware of this Reality.

Not long after that interaction, the student called again, saying that a wonderful experience had just occurred. A Voice had spoken to her the name of a man whom she had not seen for over twenty years. On hearing of this revelation, the author told her student to go to that man, and through his help, the student was able to accomplish the extraordinary and gratifying sale that she had been struggling to make for over ten years.

THE WAY

We are, in our own selves, the Way; it is always *within*. The old parable of the king and the jewel illustrates this nicely.

> A certain king came, one day, upon a beautiful gemstone, sparkling brilliantly in the clear waters of a lake. It was

clearly visible to the king, resting on the stones at the bottom of the lake, so he had the lake drained to get to it. But no gemstone was found!

As the waters returned to the lake, however, the same gem appeared, beautiful to behold, among the rocks at the bottom.

The king considered the problem and, finally, he called a servant and commanded him to climb the tall tree that grew by the side of the lake. The servant did so and found, in the thick branches, a crow's nest. And among the sticks at the bottom of that nest rested the sparkling gem. What had been seen deep in the water was only a reflection of the real thing, which was suspended above, in the opposite direction from where the king and his men had been looking.

And so it is in this dream of material existence. One feels one must seek here and there, wait for years to roll by, or find the certain people who can help us, on our way toward prosperity and happiness. Yet doing so is looking in the wrong direction; it's looking outward at the reflection, rather than inward at the Reality.

The jewel we seek is not in the outer expression. The jewel is *within*. The priceless, sparkling jewel we seek is actually our own true Self. Looking within, one sees that *always, everywhere, there is but One Being*.

Seeing and feeling this confidently, calmly, the re flection soon begins to appear in the universe (as it was in the lake) around us. But we are not deceived into thinking that what we are seeing is the Reality. We see its sparkle and rejoice in the out-picturing, the demonstration of our inner awareness, but we know that it *is* our inner awareness being reflected: the realization and the expression are inseparable. As Ralph Waldo Emerson stated in his essay, "Compensation," the seed is in the fruit; the outcome is in the action. The experience of expression is in the realization.

This, then, is the way above the path of trial, tribulation, and suffering. Our glorified thought and vision, with no mental argument, redeems us from any false sense of imperfection. We experience transcending harmony and practical demonstration by the illumination of spiritual sense, which is activated through the inspiration of the heart.

Reaching a higher sense through insight and revelation, we are able to demonstrate the Christ/Krishna/Buddha nature that is within each of us and rise effortlessly, spontaneously, into the spiritual awareness of Being, the heavenly Reality that is always present. This divine process of right interpretation, when it is acknowledged and accepted by the individual, enables each of us to subdue any material belief in sin, sickness, or limitation of any kind, and to embody the fulfillment of the Spirit that we truly Are.

We see this in all the sacred scriptures of the world. In the Christian New Testament, Jesus restored to human consciousness the lost sense of perfection and established this harmony, wholeness, joy, and happiness as the reality of our individual being. In the Hindu *Bhagavad Gita* Krishna demonstrates for his disciple, Arjuna, the unreality of the world around him and the fulfilled Reality available through spiritual insight. In the Buddha's *Sutras*, we are shown the Middle Way, beyond any sense of material excess or deprivation, into the sublime Reality of Spirit, called *Atman*, within. Likewise for the *Q'uran*, the *Tao te Ching*, and even the works of some of the ancient Greek philosophers. All tell us to seek within for the Power and Presence that lift us beyond the appearances of limitation in the world around us.

NO REAL CHANGE

And as we do so, we become aware that there is no *actual* transition from belief to understanding, from appearance to Reality, but that the ideas expressed in the words transition, resurrection, and ascension are simply ways to explain the appearance of a change by means of language.

We do not deny untrue beliefs or untrue expressions with the thought of destruction. On the contrary, we use denials with the spiritual insight and conviction that destruction is unnecessary. As Paul's letter to Timothy says, in the Christian New Testament, "The law (of destruction and punishment) is not made for a righteous man... but pray for all...." And as Krishna tells Arjuna in the *Bhagavad Gita*, "Who sees *Brahman* (the Lord) in every creature, deathlessly dwelling among the mortal; that person sees truly."

When we dream at night, we apparently move from one place to another place; we apparently change from one idea to another. But on waking, it's clear that no physical action has taken place; nothing has actually happened. It was an appearance based on our mental activity.

So it is with all our ideas about the material world; what appears is not really happening; it is an appearance based on our mental activity.

As we come to understand this, we understand further that when we put off wrong beliefs and accept true Vision, when we put off the idea and appearance of mortality and put on the actuality of our immortality, this too is only a mental activity and so only an appearance.

And so we begin to see that true experience is changeless, irresistible; it's omnipresence. Although deliverance and emancipation from erring beliefs and their resulting conditions may seem real in this dream experience, the ideas of deliverance and emancipation are merely symbols, reminding us of the freedom that is always present to us. Our Spirit-Self is truly free; it *is* Freedom.

Rising Into Full Awareness

In truth, perfect individual identity, Infinite Being, is here, now. And as we awaken to awareness and acceptance of this glorious fact, we behold our being "on earth as it is in heaven," as Jesus calls for in the New Testament. Or, as Krishna tells Arjuna in the *Bhagavad Gita,* "that person... ever aware of the Omnipresent ever about him... reaches that bliss which is highest."

Thus, in the same way as waking from a dream at night delivers us from the conditions of that dream, full awareness of our own changeless being as eternal Life brings deliverance from the dream experiences called sin, sickness, all forms of distress, and death.

In the New Testament, Jesus' final demonstration of this principle is called Ascension; having conquered the illusion of death, he rose above *all* experience of illusion. Ascension is rising into full awareness of self as Self, as Spirit, as God taking on human form while retaining all the qualities of the Creative Source and Sustainer of universes.

Full ascension, then, delivers *all* power, peace, glory, harmony, and all the other qualities of the divine. As our awareness and thought harmoniously ascend the scale of being, only the good is perceived; good's Omnipresence is fully experienced. And it's through right interpretation that we can lift our thought above the dream state to reveal the Real and True, the energetic Self, the spiritual body that is apparent in ascension.

BEYOND PERCEPTION

As the science of metaphysics (study of underlying and overarching principle) rises beyond the science of physics (study of the material world), so the Absolute Science of spiritual ascension rises above and beyond any mental practice or discipline. Through mental practice, we rise above the limitations of the body and brain, but through spiritual ascension we rise above all dreams and illusions, achieving the right and ability to experience our heritage: glorified Being.

Right interpretation is the first step beyond the illusion. Right interpretation reveals what our culturally trained materialist ego-brain self can't perceive. For example, reports that the universe is imperfect and incomplete must be false, because the universe — and everything in it — is the expression of Life, Truth, and Love, and so is as perfect, changeless, and immortal as the Intelligence, Life, Being, that sustains it.

Right interpretation sees beyond relative appearances. According to appearances, it is relatively true that a mortal is not an immortal, and relatively true that the universe beheld by unillumined vision is not Heaven. Nonetheless, one Identity is always present, whether one interprets this Identity as perfect and divine or as imperfect and incomplete. Likewise, one universe is ever-present, whether one interprets it as material and chaotic, or heavenly and glorious; it's the expression of the Source, of Life, of Spirit, and is therefore perfect and whole — spiritual substance in form.

Right interpretation of the perfect universe reveals harmonious existence at hand. Though one may call the universe matter, illusion, counterfeit, let it be clearly understood that perfect Being and the Universe are eternally One: Source and Expression; fire and flame. Thus, casting aside erring perceptions, and using our spiritual vision, we see that the universe before us is none other than the "kingdom of heaven" and every individual entity before us can only be perfect Being. Through our spiritual vision we appreciate and recognize the perfect universe — and naturally, effortlessly, experience it as such.

EACH ONE THE WAY

Over the millennia, prophets and saints have left different instructions regarding the way in which this realm of perfect harmony and immortality may be experienced. Some have suggested mental and behavioral laws: "thou shalt nots." Others have encouraged abstinence, trials, tribulations, and self-deprecation as the path. The great Masters of all traditions, however, have declared simply, "Look within for all that matters;" "The kingdom of Heaven is within you."

They're reminding us that each of us, individually, is the way to heavenly experience. How can we give living waters to the thirsty unless our own hearts are over flowing with divine glory? How can we demonstrate health and wellbeing instantaneously unless our own consciousness is inspired with the revelation of perfect Love and Life?

It's through our individual awareness, then, our recognition and acceptance of Self as God, and of the universe as expressing that perfect Self, that we enter the experience of Heaven on Earth, the glory of ascension.

In that awareness Truth is revealed. In that conscious ness, perfect Being and the perfect universe that have always been here, now, are revealed — to us and to those around us.[33]

PERFECTION EXPERIENCED

As we take such conscious possession of Reality within ourselves, we can individualize infinite power and glory in our experience. As we ascend beyond the illusions of materiality, we begin to express unlimited health, happiness, and harmony in our lives and world. It all depends on the individual viewpoint, the individual interpretation of experience. As one maintains the conviction of the presence and permanence of heavenly Reality, which is made up of the immortal principles and qualities of the Source, these qualities *must* be one's experience.

Permanent perfection, irresistible harmony, perpetual beauty, and love are the true, present qualities of the Reality of Being. So it is that, as one sets aside all mental argument, resting in the feeling and understanding of one Presence as *all that is, now and always,* instantaneous healing is demonstrated.

This means that our practical demonstration rests on our understanding of the spiritual base of our being, and this Science of the Absolute perfection of Being lifts

---

[33] It may be said that this is what the "unification" step in the 5step method of Positive Prayer, as taught in Science of Mind and Unity, is all about. We use words to enter a state of consciousness in which we know and *feel* ourselves to be unified with the Spirit-Self, Divine Mind, Source of all that is. And in that state of consciousness, we declare what we know to be True, rising above appearances and expressing and experiencing the Truth of Health, Abundance, Loving Relationships: Wellbeing in all its forms.

individual awareness to the spiritual sense of life as Life and love as Love and the world as Heaven.

Bringing out the highest phenomena of Reality in our experience, this Absolute Science is the absolute deliverer, the fulfillment of being. It's the salvation from illusion that all humanity seeks, delivering both material and spiritual health, harmony, and happiness. These are the demonstrations to which thousands can attest.

We see then, that the more fully this Science of Being, this spiritual awareness, is understood and interpreted, the higher the demonstrations experienced. To the degree that anyone accepts and uses the understanding that our real nature is the divine Trinity — Source, Power, and Presence[34] — they bring to individual experience all the glorious qualities of Heavenly Reality that our real nature actually is.

NO NEED TO DENY WHAT DOES NOT EXIST

Looking through the eyes of our cultural training, one might say that the universe is matter, illusion, counterfeit, and later may be taught another false view: the need to deny such matter, evil, falsity. Yet, as we've learned in this Science, right perception shows us that there is no need to deny a material universe, for *there is no material universe; all is spirit, perfection,* and what is nonexistent need not be denied. The only universe that

---

[34] There are many ways to express what the Christians call "Father, Son, and Holy Spirit." Each of them acknowledges that there is a Source of all that is, expressing as various forms, and continuing to create through principle and power. Some other expressions include: "Source, Substance, and Spirit;" "Mother, Child, and Love;" "Being, Expression, and Creative Power;" *"Brahman, Atman, Aum;"* and *"Consciousness, Quantum Field, Tendency.*

exists is the perfect expression of the Source: finished, complete, heavenly.

Erroneously interpreting this finished realm in which all dwell in harmony as "material," "changeable," or even "evil," prevents one from consciously experiencing the glories of Reality, and encourages reports of a false world and false experiences.

Through divine revelation, insight, and demonstration, however, the untrue view of a material world disappears, and the Reality, the spiritual ideal, the Christ/Krishna/Buddha within each of us, radiates into, and is clearly demonstrated in, our world. Through the fire of inspiration, we come to accept our true nature, and, with right interpretation of experience, the world around us reveals its ever-present harmonious, heavenly qualities.

Interpreting the universe through Truth, we see that there is no necessity nor advantage in denying matter, sin, sickness, death, for these conditions simply are not found in this heavenly realm in which we are living. The acknowledgement of the omnipresence and omnipotence of perfect, changeless, being and perfect, change less experience *includes* the only possible denial.

This spiritual action is Ascension. Here, the Self that we are begins to consciously perceive and express its glory, power, perfection, and harmony, in every aspect of being, everywhere and always.

∞

SUMMARY POINTS

- Having grown up in a world of lies and false-hoods, we are looking at life through a veil, see-ing everything inverted; now stripping off the veil of illusions we begin to perceive Truth as all Reality, and to recognize that the unreality we were taught to focus on is actually nothing.

- As waking from a dream at night delivers us from the conditions of that dream, full aware-ness of our own changeless being as eternal Life brings deliverance from the dream experiences called sin, sickness, distress, and death.

- As we set aside all mental argument, resting in the feeling and understanding of one Presence as *all that is, now and always,* instantaneous heal-ing is demonstrated.

- Nothing external is to be changed, healed, or re-moved; rather than going outward to conquer darkness or distress, we go inward only, and there we find the Truth: that we *are* Omnisci-ence, Omnipresence, Omnipotence.

- Interpreting the universe rightly, we see that there is no necessity nor advantage in denying matter, sin, sickness, death, for these conditions simply are not found in this heavenly realm in which we are living.

- While prophets and saints have left different in-structions regarding ways to experience this realm of perfect harmony and immortality, the great Masters have declared that each of us, in-dividually, is the way.

- It is through our individual recognition and ac-ceptance of Self as God, and of the universe as expressing that perfect Self, that we experience Heaven on Earth.

TO PONDER:

1. Did someone tell you that suffering is necessary or inevitable, that "no pain, no gain"? Were you taught that martyrdom is admirable? That sacrifice and tribulation is the path to holiness? Can you see that accepting those ideas, admiring those people, following their advice, has led you away from experiencing a perfect universe of perfect joy and beauty?

2. Consider a process of learning and discovering that is full of joy and wonder, like toddlers discovering something they've never seen before, or a monk entering an amazing new environment – all smiles and joyful discovery. What would your life be like if you could approach each new change or discovery with such an attitude? What could you learn if you were to experience each new idea or concept that way?

3. Sitting quietly and observing one's thoughts about things is called "revery." It used to be a normal part of life. In the Hebrew tradition it's part of Sabbath: just sitting quietly and being aware of what one is saying to oneself, what thoughts float idly by. As we do so, we find that much of what is in our "background thinking," our "default pattern" in the brain is not what's True, real, or good. So spend some time just observing your thoughts—sitting quietly or as you're driving, doing dishes or laundry, walking, or cleaning up—what is actually going on in your thinking and feeling? Then do some re

framing, releasing, replacing of those thoughts and focus the brain's activity on what you know to be True, good, and Real.

TO PRACTICE:

- Sit in a comfortable, peaceful place and allow your awareness to explore the infinity of space until your awareness recognizes and accepts your individual Self as present throughout that space.

- Acknowledge that you are the Infinite Presence in all that is and that infinite presence is what we call God.

- Accept that the universe you are contemplating is expressing the perfect Self that is, everywhere, and that your individual body-mind is, now, that perfect Self in expression.

- *Feel* that consciousness, the perfect Being and the perfect universe that have always been here, now, as your own Self.

- As you do so, allow yourself to enter the experience of Heaven on Earth – for you, and for those around you. Enjoy the experience for as long as you like, knowing that what you experience from now on must be more heavenly.

CHAPTER 6

PARADISE: HEAVEN ON EARTH

Paradise is within us. Living from our conscious ness of our unlimited health, joy, abundance, peace, comfort, immortality, is Heaven on Earth.

We are redeemed from any so-called "laws" of the material world as we *think, feel,* and *act* in the perfect Oneness. Such spiritualization of thought and senses is the practice called prayer. This is the way in which Paradise is brought into our awareness, and Soul replaces sense.

Up to now, our experience of Earth has been a plane where progress appears to happen, where increasing immunity from so-called "evil" is based on our increasing awareness of the presence of Reality, and our ability to disregard appearances that are unreal. We've depended on our ability to know Truth, to pray and treat correctly.

Now, however, we have established a foundation in our consciousness, the understanding that our individual identity is the One, Truth, eternal, and, beyond that, we have accepted that all untrue belief can be dissolved and replaced with spiritual understanding.

So, now, we begin to see how we can pray or treat in a way that deliverance from erring beliefs may be quick and certain — for ourselves and others.

EXPERIENCING TRUTH

We begin with the realization that, in order to effortlessly rise to our true nature as Spirit, in order to feel at one with the Source of All, we must appreciate that state (our own immortal beingness) and continue to experience it as our true Self. How can we rise above limitation unless we are unlimited? How can we rise in the Strength of Spirit unless we *are* Spirit? How can we execute all power unless we *are* Power? How can we dissolve erring beliefs unless we, ourselves, are Understanding?

Just as we must know that 2+2=4 to agree that 2+2 does not equal 5,[35] we must understand our *actual* being in order to understand that we are not subject to material, mortal beliefs. To say that the numbers 2 and 2 add up to 5 is equivalent to saying that anyone is a "mortal, human" being, while to say they add up to 4 is recognizing that all humanity is immortal, spiritual being. So it is that when false, or erring belief operates, the result is an appearance, an untruth; and when Truth or Understanding operate, the result is the experience of Truth.

Consider the problem set up in the Christian Bible. In the beginning (the opening lines of the book of Genesis) is God. At the end (the final lines of the book of Revelation) is God. The problem becomes: *since God is the beginning and the ending, what are we?*

Approaching this theological problem with the understanding that when false, or erring belief operates, the result is an appearance, an untruth; and when Truth or Understanding operate, the result is the experience of Truth clarifies much.

---

[35] Clearly, she is speaking of the addition of integers or whole numbers here, as those who are familiar with the rounding of fractions or decimals know that it's entirely possible to add 2.48 to 2.48 and come up with 5, because 2.48 would be "rounded down" to 2 and 4.96 would be "rounded up" to 5. The point is still valid: some principles can be applied in any situation.

AWAKENING FROM THE DREAM

When anyone believes they are a mortal human being, subject to discord and limitation, they externalize this idea in their lives and world. But, all the time, no matter whether one is seeing rightly or erringly, the answer is fixed, sure. It's like the dreaming person who is not really the being moving through the dream, whether walking happily in a mountain meadow or descending into a nightmare, yet every aspect of the dream is still in the mind of the person dreaming. Regardless of the complexity and nature of the dream, there is only one entity: the entity on the couch who has drifted off into a dream.

In our earthly existence we have heard, all around, reports of poverty, sickness, and other forms of distress. We can say "all that is a dream and doesn't exist in Reality," yet, in the same way that any dream can be traced back to the mind of a person dreaming, our limited earthly experience can be traced back to its source, a pattern of thinking that is operating on untrue beliefs.

Understanding this principle, we realize that mind is the source of our experience, and only a brain whose patterns of thought are filled with Truth[36] can experience the joyful wellbeing that is our Reality.

Just as the person in the dream is unaware that they are lying on the couch, the person on the couch, awakening from the dream, is no longer aware of being the person in the dream. Similarly, as an individual is aware that they are God-being (Self-conscious), they

---

[36] Emma Curtis Hopkins encouraged her students to "fill their thoughts and words" by speaking and thinking only of omnipresent, omnipotent Good, everywhere, all the time, as the way to bring about the transformation that leads to the experience of the intended good.

are unaware of being a material form subject to disease, discord, and all other forms of distress: the dream picture of such things is gone.

Becoming aware that our life and our being is wholly Spirit, what we call God (for there is no other Life, no other Spirit), we are Self-aware. This process, which we call "spiritual healing," is one in which our thought ascends and old material beliefs yield to spiritual understanding.

RETURNING TO OUR SOURCE

In the laws of physics, water may flow only as high as its source. Likewise, our awareness may flow as high as our Source, and if we spiritual beings are to return to our true Home, our Source, we must understand what that is.

We must recognize that we already are the perfection we seek to return to, that we already are the same substance and mind as our Source.

The person on the couch, dreaming, can only rise as high within the dream as the normal patterns of thought in the brain that is dreaming, and, the instant the dreamer is aware of the body on the couch, they are no longer in the dream. In the same way, those of us who are dreaming this life in the natural universe are awakening from that dream. We realize that we have been in a dream of separation, but the one dreaming is the one universal mind, the God-mind that is our true mind. We realize that our sense of self, our individualized expression of that God-mind, is simply a dream of possibilities. And as we do so, we awaken to our true Oneness, and the dream of separation ceases.

DISSOLVING THE PARADOX

This means that if we identify with the Prodigal child, returning home, we are confronted with the paradox of returning to a "land" from which we never left. Spiritual teachers have tried to help us understand this for millennia. Rumi tells us, "all that you want is inside you," and the New Testament gospels say, "The Kingdom is within you."

The paradox dissolves, however, when we realize it's simply a problem of putting off the dream, the untruth, and putting on the true, the Reality. The belief that we are isolated, mortal beings, subject to distress and death, is the untrue myth; it's the dream state from which we are to awaken.

The person on the couch need not assert the fact of lying on the couch, for this is obvious. But the self that is dreaming wanders on foreign streets and, tired and weary, wishes to return to house and home, to rest on the couch, where the body is already resting. All that is needed, then, is for the dreamer to assert the truth — rest and freedom from the tiresome streets — asserting it in the name of,[37] which is to say identifying with, the person dreaming, rather than the person in the streets. With a "No! I am *not* actually stuck in this situation! I am dreaming!" the dream images vanish and all that

---

[37] When Jesus, in the New Testament, says to ask or pray "in my name," it means to identify with, to enter into the nature of, the Christ mind. The word "name" is translated from *shem*, which in Hebrew and Aramaic, means the essence of, the qualities of, the characteristic nature of, not just the sounds or letters of a given name. This is why argument among Bible-based Christians about what name to use in prayer is moot. This is also part of why the Jews do not (cannot) speak the name of God — and why the Taoist says "that which can be named is not the Tao." It's a state of being, not a word.

remains is the person on the couch with a vague memory of having dreamt.

Similarly, people who have believed they are limited and mortal, who feel the need for health and harmony, can simply assert — while in the dream of mortal existence — their true identity, their freedom from all forms of distress. They are the mind that is dreaming. Let them declare it "No! I am not stuck in this limitation! I am the Source of the dream, the mind that is dreaming a limited experience!" And lo! The dream vanishes and what remains is the one Mind, the one Presence, the Spirit, Buddha Nature, Christ Mind, *Atman,* Who we all truly are.

So it is that, while we seem to be in the dream of material existence, as "mortals," we need only to assert our freedom in the name of, identifying with, the God being (called Christ, Buddha, Spirit, *Atman,* or whatever name is familiar) that we actually are. For what other is there? Spirit is all, so nothing else exists. This name, the essence of our being (Christ, Buddha, Spirit, *Atman,* or Krishna nature), is written in our cells. Joyfully we claim it; we believe it; we accept it.

When the one dreaming of foreign lands realizes they are on the couch, they experience rest and repose. And when we realize we have been dreaming of being mortals in a limited world, we awaken to our true Life of glory and immortality.

EXPERIENCING TRUTH

When our deepest convictions are founded in Truth, we experience Truth supporting us, and we accept the power of Truth as the only thing that can undo the effects of errant thoughts and dreams. We then begin to experience the power of Truth at work in our lives. Our senses are awakened to the reality of our Spirit Self in a heavenly Life; we see the mortal self and limited world as the dream that it truly is.

In performing a treatment, we are accepting Truth, our freedom as spiritual beings. A real, spiritual being cannot be sick, and most certainly an unreal, dream being cannot be sick. For someone to know that they are a real, spiritual being is for that person to experience a body that utters no complaints. This is what the apostle Paul meant when he wrote to the Roman Christians, "the Spirit bears witness with our spirit."

The beginning of wisdom is, therefore, the understanding of self as Spirit. Accepting this reality, one spontaneously rises to new heights of experience, in which self becomes Self, one with the Universe in its spiritual perfection.[38]

Absolute Science, then, is the means by which we come to this realization. It reveals to us that Omnipotence is enthroned in the heart of all beings, and must be (ultimately *can't not* be) acknowledged and demonstrated by all beings. As we practice this Science and come to accept Truth as the basis for our convictions, all dreams of limits fall away; doors that appeared closed are open or nonexistent; bodies that appeared damaged are seen to be strong and whole. The light of true wisdom surrounds all beings and all is glorified, and the earth and heaven become one heavenly realm,

---

[38] This is the experience common to all those whose brain and body are "flatlined" and declared dead, then, after minutes or hours, come back to tell what they saw, felt, and heard: the realization of self as not a body, but as unlimited spirit, expanded across space and time, coming back to occupy a body. (We call them "Near Death Experiences.")

because our Christ/Buddha/Krishna nature has become our experience.

All the prophecies are fulfilled in us as we accept Truth as the basis of our understanding. We ascend from sense to glory, from belief to power, from cross to crown.

And that crown no one can take from us for it's our own spiritual understanding, encrusted with the jewels that adorn the New Jerusalem (which means the new "place of peace"), the shining divine qualities that are the aspects of all being.[39]

Our new understanding shines like a beacon, lighting our way, guiding us through an experience of heavenly qualities, of constantly expanding opportunities and resources, and out of any sense experience of limitation, lack, or distress.

So let us, now, let go of any ideas of trial or tribulation, knowing them to be the dream of a past that doesn't exist. Let us accept, instead, the crown of enlightened understanding, resting in the peace and power of Truth as our reality.

THE HEAVENLY LIFE OF SELF

If there is no possibility of separation from the Source of All, there is no being separate from the One and no partition within the One, which means no self exists but the One Self. And if all that exists is the expression of the One Truth, Life, and Love, then the body that exists *must be perfect, ideal, and glorious.*

---

[39] These jewels are described by Emma Curtis Hopkins in her book *High Mysticism*, and explained in Ruth Miller's *Unveiling Your Hidden Power.*

This recognition of self as Soul, Spirit, Life, Truth, Love, strikes the note of universal freedom. We rest in the peace of conscious strength and power. As we do so, the universe is no longer seen as "out there" and "dangerous," but understood to be an extension, an expression of our very own Self, demonstrating the infinite glories and potentials of our beingness.[40]

We do not give up the body; we give up false ideas of the body. "Healing" therefore, becomes simply true insight, or realization of the Truth of the wholeness and wellbeing of all life forms, all bodies, all situations. The practitioner changes nothing, but simply brings to awareness the Truth that is already there: the perfection, the glory, of the Real Self.

What was called in the New Testament "casting out demons" is now understood as simply turning away from false beliefs, letting go of erring ideas—for ourselves and others. We let go of old attachments to the cross, to trials and tribulations, and accept the crown of enlightened understanding that is the New Testament "Christ in you, the hope of glory," or the Hindu "Self that is immanent in Nature, which transcends Nature and which is the Absolute."

As we give up false ideas about the body, we understand "raising the dead" as the experience of uninterrupted peace and unconditional love surrounding us in a harmonious environment, forever. We do not give up pleasure, companionship, enjoyable activities; we give up all false ideas about what constitutes—and are

---

[40] The James Webb Space Telescope is doing just that. Many false ideas about the universe are being dissolved in the presence of its glorious images of ancient stars and galaxies in a universe that, so far as we can measure, has no clear beginning or edge.

the consequences of — pleasure, companionship, and enjoy able activities. We realize that *Paradise is nothing other than the acceptance and experience of our actual identity.*

With spiritual vision we behold paradise as our reality, here and now. This is the "good news" (which is what the word *gospel* means): the continual presence of unchanging Good, the ever-present heavenly Reality, experienced as happiness, harmony, health — on earth as it is in heaven.

THE CLAIM

Truth brings its own peace and harmony, delivering its own joy, inspiration, and uplift. Truth says

> You cannot come into My presence without acknowledging me as the one and only power and reality. And this is life eternal.

This is life eternal, that we recognize and know our reality and *our identity* as the One, the only Source and Substance of all.

Claiming our identity with the Source, the Spirit that enlivens all, we begin to have ideas and visions that are harmonious with the Spirit, and begin to align body, mind, and emotions with the One power and presence that is, always and everywhere.

As we acknowledge ourselves as free, unfettered, flawless, triumphant, we acknowledge the world around us, our universe, as heavenly, glorious, radiant. Acknowledging that we, ourselves, are Truth, triumphant, we strike the note of ever higher achievements. We are strong beyond the strength of the body, wise above the power of mentality, radiating a peace and harmony that transcends all earthly experience.

So let yourself envision, think, and act from the standpoint of your divinity. Use spiritual texts to uplift the awareness and quicken the fire within as needed; a lighted consciousness transmits illumination.

RISEN CONSCIOUSNESS

We place ourselves above our thoughts and are spontaneously lifted to greater heights of knowledge and understanding. Transcending the cultural belief in limitation and bondage, all trace of that so-called limitation or bondage disappears. No longer placing ourselves under the action of thought and its consequences, we are no longer hindered by them.

Rising to the awareness of our full dominion in Spirit, into the Christ/Buddha/Krishna consciousness, we are glorified in our God-being. We begin to experience our lives as the constant and absolute Good that is our true Reality. As the one Source that we call God is changeless, we are changeless Reality, not subject to the ups and downs of human experience or earthly life. We find ourself living in the only true Reality, the Real Universe, which we call heaven.

This sublime consciousness bridges over the periods called, birth, aging, and death. Seeing that there is no departure nor lapse from perfection, and therefore no return to perfection, we discover that we have already arrived, that we are perfect, without the process of progression.

In the full consciousness of our immortality and glory we claim:

I am the flame. I am the inspiration.

I am the finished wholeness and completion. I am awake, alive, forevermore.

Nothing—no thought, words, or experience— can

separate me from the beingness that I Am,
for I am, now and forever, all that I have called God: the
Source, Spirit, and Substance of all that is.

In this uplifted awareness we realize that all things
that were possible to Christ Jesus in the New Testament
are possible to us, now. All that Krishna and the gods
of the Vedas could do, we can do. In this awareness,
with this insight, we experience the ultimate understanding, the ascension — the *experience* of supernal harmony, bliss, immortality.

Always, everywhere, there is only one entity in one
expression. Know this.

We are the dreamless, the ageless, the deathless Reality.
We are the all-conquering, self-existing, unchangeable expressions of the One Source of all being.

∞

SUMMARY POINTS

- Living from our consciousness of our unlimited
  health, joy, abundance, peace, comfort, immortality, is Heaven on Earth.

- We are redeemed from any so-called "laws" of
  the material world as we *think, feel,* and *act* in the
  perfect Oneness, which process is called prayer.

- Those of us who have been dreaming this life in
  the natural universe are awakening from the
  dream and realizing the Truth of our Self.

- When our deepest convictions are founded in
  Truth, we experience Truth supporting us, all
  dreams of limits fall away; doors that appeared
  closed are open or nonexistent; bodies that appeared damaged are seen to be strong and
  whole.

- There is no possibility of separation from the Source of All, no being separate from the One, and no partition within the One, so no self exists but the One Self, and the body that exists *must be perfect, ideal, and glorious.*

- No longer placing ourselves under the action of culturally entrained thought and its consequences, we are no longer hindered by them.

- The universe is not seen as "out there" and "dangerous," but understood to be an extension, an expression of our very own Self, demonstrating our infinite glories and potentials.

- Claiming our identity with the Spirit that enlivens all, we begin to have ideas and visions that are harmonious with Spirit, and align body, mind, and emotions with the One power and presence.

- In this uplifted awareness we realize that all things that were possible to Christ Jesus in the New Testament are possible to us, now. All that Krishna and the gods of all spiritual traditions could do, we can do.

TO PONDER:

1. Remember a time when you were "in the flow," without thought about what you need to do or how, and everything unfolded effortlessly. Imagine life being always like that.

2. When you do a treatment, you can feel the Power, and may even feel as if the Presence of Spirit is speaking and working through and as you. What would life be like if every moment

were that?

3. Consider some people or situations that you have thought of as less than perfect. Imagine their perfection – seeing, hearing, touching the whole and perfect Reality of each one.

TO PRACTICE:

- Sit in a comfortable place and imagine living in this world with no sense of separation. Imagine that you are not separate from the animals, the insects, the plants, the rocks – they are all You, aspects of yourself, showing up in just the way you called them forth.
- Now take a walk around your home, seeing everyone and everything you encounter as your own Self showing up in just the way you called them forth.
- Now go shopping, or to church, or to a restaurant with the same idea in mind.
- Write down what you're experiencing and how you have changed as a result.

CHAPTER 7

ROLLING AWAY THE STONE

There's an ancient story that provides a powerful insight. In it,

A person spends a lifetime searching for a particular jewel. Day after day, year after year, every resource is spent seeking it.

One day, a trusted friend hands that person a velvet box saying, "In this box, you will find that for which you have long been searching. Here is the jewel of your heart."

The first thing that happens to the seeker is awe and wonder, and then a sense of peace. The search is over. There is no hurry to open the box. It is here; that is enough.

Perhaps someone now reading these lines has been dealing with problems, fears, troubles. That which you've been seeking seems far off and unattainable.

Let this message, the *Science of Ascension*, be the precious Jewel, the priceless Treasure, delivered into your hand. It is here. Yours.

There's no need to hurry or accomplish anything. No need to rush to overthrow past thoughts of sickness, sin, worry, or limitation. You can now relax and be at peace, for your heart has seen the Light, the Truth of Heaven at hand.

This Truth means effortless freedom from any past material experiences and concerns. It means an awareness that is divine, a mind that is no longer darkened by past misunderstandings but is lighted by the Light of Wisdom and Joy.

Your Jewel is here. The mystery is unveiled. Now you see the Way, you feel the joy and receive the glory that Infinite Consciousness has prepared for those who arise and accept the Way to the perfection that in actuality, you never left. And into your experience comes a new heaven and a new earth, brought forth by your Understanding—as old beliefs about a heaven separate from earth have been dissolved.

Because we have abolished the belief that we are limited human beings and have accepted that we are Spirit in form, we are prepared to accept the glories of Ascension. As Spirit, God-being, we cannot be sick and we cannot die. Our eyes now see and our ears now hear the wonderful things and glorious vision that have always been prepared for us.

VARYING EXPERIENCES

Often people ask why it is that some students comprehend and accept advanced ideas of Truth readily and easily, while others, apparently equally as eager and earnest, do not accept them—instead holding tenaciously to different views and concepts.

The process of individual acceptance is illustrated in the following.

A group of friends enter a new, beautifully furnished home to examine its style, furniture, art, and other aspects of its design and décor. In this group are an electrician, an artist, a musician, and some children of varying ages.

They all enter the spacious and luxurious home. Does the musician give his attention immediately to the tapestries, the decorated ceiling, the flooring? No, indeed. The grand piano is all that the musician is immediately aware of, and the other instruments alongside it. Does the artist focus on the piano as well? By no means! The paintings, etchings, and handmade objects that may be found in every room command the artist's attention. The electrician, of course, is intrigued with the latest electrical fixtures and appliances. The children, then, amuse themselves with whatever books and gadgets appeal to them while the adults are focused elsewhere.

Now, everything about this group of people is just as it should be at that moment. Each of them is following their own inclination and is finding pleasure and satisfaction in their particular focus.

It's the same for the great number of people who study the various sacred scriptures and metaphysical texts. Year after year we can find books written by fine, educated minds that set out to prove various aspects of scripture to be true or false – based on points drawn from the same texts. Each person has simply expressed their own individual state of consciousness, using the texts to support the opinions arising from that state.

There are as many points of view as there are individuals. Each one sees and hears according to their current state of consciousness, and so is able to draw from the same material very different conclusions.

Yet the person who has chosen to live by faith, rather than intellectual argument, is not dismayed by these seeming contradictions. We realize that, as we have climbed the ladder of life, we have chosen what we shall see and believe, but we reach a point where we no longer choose, no longer distinguish, no longer adopt certain sets of beliefs. At this point the apparent paradox of multiple interpretations is resolved: *we see on all sides and reconcile all as One –all views blend into one great Reality.*

From this point we can understand another's view, no matter where they stand upon the ladder of life – and we can show others the next step ahead. Anyone studying life has a right to think and act according to their viewpoint. What else can they do?

As a result, during the transition period, when old beliefs and thought processes are in force, when one is still choosing, selecting, balancing, arguing, separating, and dividing, everyone acts according to their unfolding views.

At that stage in development, the individual is seeing two factors, two sides of life, and is choosing between them.

Then, as their studies progress, their experience is broadened, and they reach a level of understanding — perhaps slowly, perhaps swiftly – where the apparent paradox is resolved. At this point, each one exclaims, with the ancient prophets: "The darkness and light are the same!"

From this point on, only Oneness is perceived. As the individual looks around, at the office, in books, on the screen, in the stars – lo! Everything speaks of *One* life, *One* being, *One* expression.

Now it becomes clear why the words Unity, agreement, cooperation, harmony, and peace are heard everywhere. Down through the ages, the words *"Let there be light!"* resound. And now, multitudes are hearing the sound and following the vision it holds.

With the dawning of awareness of this oneness and indivisibility, we are gently lifted from a mortal, limited state of thinking to a free, immortal state of understanding. We leap from perception and projection to a simple, direct knowledge, without the need to reason things out. In this awareness we see the heavenly new earth, for there is no longer any idea of separation, Since our experience always corresponds to our state of consciousness, we are now living the command of

Jesus' famous prayer: "Thy will be done on Earth as it is in Heaven.".

ALL IS ONE, NOW

"That which has been is now; and that which is to be has already been" says the biblical prophet.[41] Every good thing that seems to be coming *to us* is already here. It's simply coming into our individual recognition. Although it's being apprehended by our individual consciousness now, in Reality it has been here from Eternity. Creation, then, is a process of constantly and eternally appearing to individual recognition.

In Truth, in Reality, the "Kingdom of the Father" is not just coming, *it is here* — on earth as it is in Heaven. This means that, for each of us, as awareness of the indivisible One dawns, light arrives and darkness is ended. All over the earth, the end of separation, opposition, ignorance, division, becomes apparent. For the Light of Reality is here; illumination consumes all misunderstanding. The One Love lives in the hearts of individuals, in their social groups and institutions, and in all the nations, Now.

What good is it for the Self to be God — almighty, unlimited, glorious — if we don't let this One *shine* in us? If we don't let it *act* in, through, and *as* us?

In order to experience the reality of our freedom and authority, let's accept and practice the One Presence as All. In this way, whatever has seemed false in our minds will be transcended, swallowed up by the divine Good in our own, true nature.

---

[41] Ecclesiastes 3:15 in the Hebrew Bible (also called *Tanakh*) and Christian Old Testament

As we perceive the allness of the One and the oneness of the All, we can join with the angels in saying "Glory in the highest and peace on earth."[42] We join the biblical prophets in saying "the desert blossoms as the rose; the lion and the lamb express the same being."[43] We join the New Testament Jesus in saying "I and the Father (Source and Provider) are One."[44] And "I am the alpha and omega; the beginning and the end."[45] We join the Hindu Krishna in saying

> I am the father of the universe and its mother, essence and goal of all knowledge,
>
> the refiner, the sacred Om, and the threefold Vedas.
>
> I am the beginning and the end, origin and dissolution,
>
> refuge, home...[46]

Feeling Truth in us and as us, it must be so.

There's always a way beyond intellectual understanding and experience. The caterpillar may wish it could fly, but will not be able to do so until and unless it accepts and allows an incomprehensible process to transform it into the butterfly or moth that its genes are programmed to become.

So it is for humans who wish to experience limitless freedom. We must accept and allow a process that is far beyond the capacity of logic or reason to understand. Indeed, the process we are to go through requires putting aside all attempts at reasoning or understanding,

---

[42] In the Christian New Testament descriptions (Matthew and Luke) of the angels announcing the birth of the Christ.

[43] Paraphrasing the prophet Isaiah in the Hebrew *Tanakh* and Christian Old Testament.

[44] John 10:30 in the New Testament

[45] Revelation 22:10 in the New Testament

[46] In the *Bhagavad Gita*

for these are based on the false, limiting beliefs of the intellect, rather than the unlimited Power of the One Mind that works in and through our bodies and souls as Spirit, Life, Love, Omniscience. If we are to be free, we must put aside all reliance on visible matter and accept the unseen Spirit as our Source and Supply.

We must (meaning we ultimately will) identify ourselves with and as the Spirit-Self that we have always been, the creator and sustainer of our lives and our world, the joy-filled expression of the Love and Light that is the essence (the "beingness") of All That Is.

In that moment we know what has always been true: we ARE the Essence, the Life, the Love, that empowers and is constantly bringing forth this world. And we are totally free, not limited in any way by the creation we have brought — and are bringing — forth.

Now we realize that the God who heals, who delivers, to whom we have looked and prayed is, truly, our very own being – the Self of each of us, of all of us, of you, of me; it's the one and only Self, one Being, one Totality, one "I am." To feel this, see this, *know* this, we must interpret all experience as spiritual; we must feel and know that we, now, manifest the divine Mind, which comprises the infinitude of Truth.

And, as life is spiritually interpreted, material senses are put aside for the spiritual Science. A transition from a lower or human sense of life to a higher awareness of being occurs. This transition is the way of fulfillment through earthly development. This is what the Sufi saint, Rumi, invites us to experience:

...let's go home.
All the reasons offered by the sensible, dull, and sorrowful can't darken our hearts now ...

Don't ask too many "hows" or "whys" …
Come home to the real celebration and music.

It's also what Jesus embodies in the New Testament gospel stories. In those stories, the infant is born in the darkest hour. That infant is spiritual awareness, inspiration, born in our own inner darkness. Moving through those stories we are invited to let that inspiration shine, for it's what individualizes spiritual power; it sweeps away clouded senses, just as a breeze sweeps away the mist.

It does so as we accept the power of almighty Truth, and speak imperatively from the basis of *that* knowledge, that unyielding faith. For what we have faith in is what we have accepted deep down in our awareness, what we are counting on and expecting to be so. And when we feel that level of knowing we confidently command circumstances to bring that expectation into our experience — just as we turn on a light switch or strike a note on the piano with the full expectation that what we intend will be experienced.

In that faith, what is claimed must occur. Whatever seeming obstacle may be in the way — whatever "stone" seems to block the way — must be rolled away. The fire of our certainty, flaming with absolute Authority, dissolves all impediments. After all, what obstacle can withstand Omnipotence?

QUALITIES OF THE ASCENSION

Every advance in our spiritual development delivers a higher and clearer interpretation of Being. As the vision of Truth becomes more fully understood and practiced, individuals rise naturally and easily to the mount of Revelation. Thought soars above false beliefs to a marvelous freedom, with an indescribable love, light, and glory. Along the way, translating things into ideas and ideas into Spirit requires a higher expression to convey the higher understanding and make our commands practical. So, a "new tongue" accompanies our new, more accurate interpretation.

Our daily experience of humanity provides plenty of opportunities to express the power of Truth that is always present, but not always clear to the uninformed. *By exercising this power one advances rapidly in spiritual vision* — and achieves the mountaintop revelation of Truth and Love that is our destiny.

The view from this mountain peak seems quite different from the view in the valley. From the mount of Vision one views the universe clearly, while from the valley of perception one perceives through the erring senses and interprets the world in imperfect terms. Looking from the valley one saw issues, problems to be addressed, and progress, advancement, and the potential for regeneration – that as seeds become plants, mortals become immortals through their spiritualization and associated regeneration. Looking from the higher understanding, however, one sees that Heaven has already come to earth, that perfection of wellbeing, wholeness, fulfillment, and all the joy that comes with it, are already established – without beginning and without end, always and everywhere.

From the valley of perception, relying on the senses and their interpretation within the culture's training, one sees the universe through a mist or veil, and it only becomes clear step-by-step, as the veil is lifted through our increasing understanding. We perceive, for example, "healing" as the body changing from sickness to

health, and the manifestation of absolute Life as immortalizing the body.

One cannot, however, immortalize the body; that
has already been accomplished. The body is perfect and
whole now, and can be experienced as such when
viewed from the mountain peak of Vision, rather than
the valley of the senses.

So we must *roll away the stone of erring thoughts.* As
we accept the biblical adage, "Behold! I make all things
new!" into our awareness comes a new sense, a feeling
of joyous inspiration and strength. Now we know that,
while there is nothing to be done or outwardly accomplished, *there is an inner viewpoint that shall be attained.*
And as this viewpoint is attained, we express and experience Truth continually.

With clear vision, all is interpreted as Truth. And
in Truth, there are not two beings, one spiritual and
one material, nor two worlds, one perfect and one imperfect. It's only when we see through our previous beliefs, the perceptual framework we were given by our
culture, that we experience such divisions. The sensory
apparatus of the brain is trained to name, divide, and
categorize, while the field of mind, our true nature and
guide, apprehends the whole in all its relationships; it
speaks only of a perfect universe and life.

Our goal, therefore, has always been to retrain the
brain to follow the mind. As the great physicist, Albert
Einstein, famously said: "The intellect is our servant."
We must let go of past beliefs and thoughts that have
directed and misinterpreted our perceptions. And, as
we do so, we experience the insight and inspiration that
is always available to us, but has been blocked by our
erring beliefs and thoughts.

Then, once we experience that insight, that inspiration, we joyously accept it and we love life and all the activities of a perfect world in a glorious universe.

A PERFECT VIEW

Now, as we gain a clearer and clearer view of this perfect expression, it seems as if we're actually immortalizing and perfecting the body, but no. We are perfecting our *viewpoint*; that is all. We are establishing ourselves on the mountain peak and seeing life spiritually, rather than dwelling in the valley and interpreting life materially.

Proportionally, as we widen our horizon, we can more correctly view and interpret the perfect, complete being, and the perfect, complete universe. No change ever takes place in perfect, established being, or in perfect, established expression. Our prerogative is to know this sublime reality and to apprehend this fact of being. The ancient spiritual teachers clearly knew this. The New Testament Jesus continually reminded his followers that this perfect state, this "kingdom of heaven" is always present, "at hand." He saw the perfect expression of the One as ever-present, in all people and situations, which what his followers described as his "healings" demonstrated. This perfection is the core of spiritual stories in all the major world traditions – the perfect being is not seen or understood as such until, after a transformative event, the seeing and understanding happens.

Whether people view perfection or discord is a matter of their state of consciousness. If it happens that one person is viewing a situation from this mountain peak of perfection while another is seeing it through the material senses, then their reports may seem to contradict each other. The one viewing from the peak experiences only the perfected glory, while the other, seeing from the valley of material senses, may perceive various forms of discord and distress.

But we must understand—we must *know*—that there is no opposition to the perfection of the whole; no discord opposes harmony; no disease opposes wellbeing; no bondage opposes freedom; no death opposes life; no fear opposes love. As there is no separation in the One whole beingness that Is, there can be no opposites.

If one were to enter a dimly lit room and mistake a pedestal for an intruder, wouldn't it be absurd to insist that the imagined intruder is real, and the opposite of a real pedestal? In the same way, we would never say that heaven contradicts earth, for from the mountain peak of our spiritual insight, we can see that they are one. The material experience (perceived through the culturally programmed senses) is never the opposite of the revealed and *known* spiritual Reality. For the spiritual Reality is the *only* reality; no other state of being actually can *be*; for Reality is *all*, and is forever established throughout all the possible universes.

A New Language

So let us remove from our vocabulary any terms, words, or expressions that seem to suggest such possibilities, that suggest anything other than wholeness, perfection, peace, and harmony, for nothing other than these exist, anywhere. Let us speak in a new tongue, using a new vocabulary – one which harmonizes with the divine viewpoint of that mountain peak.

The more one thinks and speaks in the language of the One, the more quickly that person experiences the harmony of the mountain peak, with its perfect view and glorious experience.

It makes perfect sense when one considers it. Why waste time that could be spent in the glory of the One describing discord and distress? Why be concerned with one's progress along the path? Why not turn, instead, to the glorious experience, the "marriage feast," that is already prepared for us?

As we apprehend and experience the One that Is, then words like "evil" and "unhappy" and "disease" and "distress" are simply dropped from our vocabulary. As we live from this new place of being, this new state of consciousness, previous ideas and expressions describing unrealities simply and naturally fall away from our thoughts and conversations, without any effort on our part.

As mistaken ideas fall away, we experience the heavenly Reality more fully and clearly. Those viewing from the valley of material senses may call this a healing, but from the mountain peak of direct knowing, there is nothing to be healed or improved. With our spiritual vision we realize that there is no restoration of the body, simply the lifting of our sense of it to that place where we experience its already-existing wholeness and perfection. This is accomplished by calmly and trustingly, faithfully, declaring the Truth of our being:

- good is ever present;
- there are no opposites in being;
- one Presence is all that Is,
- our life and experience are the expression of the perfection of the one Presence that is, always and everywhere.

For so it truly is.

THE CALL TO OUR TRUE SELVES

Every living thing enjoys freedom. Birds and animals and high-souled humans love great forests and unwalled spaces. All living things delight in freedom because Life itself *is* Freedom.

All living things are Life, and cling to the experience of living. For example, no matter how many years someone has been in this world, even at the end there is the wish to stay a little longer, to prolong the time with loved ones. Why is this? Because the Soul, our self-identity cannot consider endings; destruction is inconceivable.

Life knows no such thing as death, and in its individual activity *cannot* be separated. Therefore, the Soul experiences no sense of separation; the passing of the body is simply a sense of rediscovering the Love-Light that *is* Life. The joys and pleasures of the world, then, are understood as mere shadows of the satisfaction that awaits us in that higher realm of being where the body is no longer limiting us.

Then, according to those who have been declared medically dead but have risen to tell of their experiences, it becomes clear that all the seeking in this world for material pleasures are, in Truth, the Soul seeking to experience what it knows to be Reality; seeking the Truth that is our only satisfaction, the Self that we *are*. The boundless freedom of that experience demonstrates to those who remember it the limitlessness of our own selves. This, then, leads to the realization that, as limitless beings we can never be satisfied with anything less than the eternal, the infinite. We may think we seek companionship, abundant supply, freedom, but what we are called to is the Unchangeable, Eternal Infinity.

And seeking that, no one will ever rest until they find it. We all must come face to face with our own glory; no amount of material wealth or supply will satisfy. There is no Having; there is only Being the Reality of the One.

In some peoples' terms this experience of becoming is called Evolution. In others, Progress. But as we rise above the limitations of language, we realize we are simply viewing the Real Self, our own divinity.

As we give ourselves to the One, the personality – that sense of being an isolated individual – dissolves. The One is our Life and our Heart; it is who we Are and always shall be.

In this way we discover that we are here for a greater destiny than to function in time and space. We become aware that the One in All is our own Self. We love people, friends, companions, relatives, not because we are attached to them, but because we see in them the Self that we all are. We become conscious of our Omnipresence, that we can instantly experience any place in time or space that we choose. We become aware of our Omniscience, that we can know anything from anywhere in space or time, instantaneously, without effort. We open to our Omnipotence, that we merely speak the Word and it is so in our world – and everywhere, across all space and all time.

Whatever seems to be a tomb enclosing someone in darkness and night, a song of praise can unblock. If we feel burdened by matter and mind, if we discover an old belief in the hardness of human problems, we rise up and sing. We sing a new song of praise, and so lift ourselves above our problems. We sing praise for Life in its wonderful freshness and everlasting loveliness. We sing praise for limitless Intelligence providing a constant flow of ideas and ordering all things divinely. We sing praise for unbounded Love with its ever-flowing affection and forgiveness. We sing praises of Truth for its overflowing abundance of supply and support. We sing until we *feel* the answer within us, the warmth and glory of our own peace and power. All song inspires and lifts the mind so that seeming troubles begin to appear smaller and further away. It dissolves all false beliefs, rolling away the stone of ignorance that has blocked the mind from experiencing the Light that Is.

The New Testament Jesus, coming to the tomb of his friend, told the villagers, "Roll away the stone!" By the power of the Word alone, in praise and thanksgiving that all he required was always answered, Jesus was able to reproduce the presence of Lazarus so that the man walked forth from the darkness into the light of his family and friends' comfort and love.

Jesus saw more, too – that all humanity could do the same. In the mind of every individual is this all-knowing Power to roll away any stone or obstacle. He saw it so clearly that, for those who were unaware that such was possible, who had never felt the Power or the Presence, he said they could simply "believe in me," which is to say "believe that I can do it with you and for you." He knew that if they could not believe in their own Self, they could, because of what they'd seen or heard him do, believe in the One that he embodied, the Christ Mind, the Universal I Am.

So, now, begin at once to believe in this Christ Mind as *your own Self*. Through accepting, believing, expecting, praising, we reach that Understanding which is able to do all things for us.

Awareness is key. We are conscious of our hands and feet; why not be conscious also of our Life and Soul? Or our superconscious mind? That which different traditions call by many names: *Atman, Father, Allah, Goddess*, and more? What Emilie Cady[47] and others call our "own Lord"? Whatever we call it, we need to be aware of the *one Reality*, the *one Being* that Is in and expressing through all.

LEARNING THE SCIENCE

Through the understanding and practice of this Science of Ascension, you will replace error with Truth, sense with Soul, and belief with Understanding. We always receive that which we know ourselves to be; so, as anyone begins to see themselves as the Trinity, to know themselves to be the Light and the Way, that person becomes fearless and free, for only Light, only Love, only the Peace and Wisdom that we now know ourselves to be can be our experience.

From beginning to end, from eternity to eternity, we are each and all destined to come into the realization that what's called "the kingdom of God" is ours, that the One actual Being is who we are. It is predestined; at some time in the experience of every individual, the false sense must be seen as not real, and true Awareness is found to be complete and ever-present.

---

[47] H. Emilie Cady in *Lessons In Truth*, published by Unity Press as the foundation text for Unity churches.

When we can look upon everyone "out there" as our own self; when we can bless all peoples' efforts to experience good as attempts to bring Heaven on Earth, then we are practicing clear vision. Then we are rolling away the stone that once held us in darkness and stepping into the light of our own glory.

Let us say,

All the good I ever thought, all the good I ever said or did or had, this good was not of my own small, self, but was Spirit working in, through, and as me. I let the universe take it; I let all who will take it – for what is Spiritual is universal – with no attachment and no will but the universal will of Love.

And as we have thus given freely, so shall we freely receive. This Science of Reality provides all good, all nourishment, all support, its Light dissolving any sense of lack, distress, disease, or discord. And the words we speak, the good that we do, will be so wonderful, so great in Love and Understanding, that our very sense of personal self will be dissolved into the universal Self that is our true nature. Then shall we see the Reality of the original unfolding that we call Creation, which is perfect and good and beautiful. Then, indeed, is our Self glorified.

Every step we take as Spirit places us more firmly and surely in the Reality of conscious joy and glory. Our bodies and minds are effortlessly carried into a greater experience of freedom and fulfillment as we accept and acknowledge the Truth of our being as Unlimited, Adorable, and Eternal. Steadily, firmly now, we keep our thoughts on the Reality of one Substance, one Power, one Life, one Being.

All that is relinquished is a material sense of life and the universe, which happens automatically as we accept and realize our actual Being and heritage. Material sense yields to the Truth of the Science of Ascension—the insight and understanding of Oneness—and does so in direct proportion as we learn and practice the radiance of our free, flawless Self.

THE EXPERIENCE

It has been said that the process of spiritual development can be described in 3 phrases:

1. "God is there" doing things to me and for me;
2. "God is here" doing things with me and through me;
3. "I am everything that I've been calling God."

Ascension, then, is the journey from sense to Soul, the felt experience of union with Spirit, the exercise of our inherent glory.

All things relevant to our Being are brought to our awareness, transcending the evidence of material senses and translating sounds and sights back into their original spiritual substance. We spiritualize thought and action. We experience direct, "face-to-face" communion with the Loving Source of all, as Revelation, free of the limitations of language or perception, while being totally understood and clear.

Indeed, a "new tongue" rapidly comes into our experience, based in the Reality of spiritual Understanding rather than the limitations of material sensations.

All consciousness, previously held in the false sense of existence, is uplifted, purified, elevated. As we accept spiritual Understanding, then divine Consciousness is found to be the only Mind, Intelligence, and Actuality, throughout all that Is.

What was called Heaven becomes our earthly experience – the "new heaven and new earth," prophesied by John in the New Testament *Revelation*, emerges as one, when the old views and former conditions pass away.

As you accept the Truth of the joys and glories of your real being, your true Understanding rolls away the stone of materialism and opens the way to the supernal delights that are your inherent nature. You can achieve *all* good, *all* joy, *all* happiness, here, now, on Earth. Seek first true Understanding of Reality (what Jesus in the New Testament called "the kingdom of Heaven") and the abundance of infinite harmonies, pleasures, and glories must be showered upon you, in all aspects of your experience. Such is the nature of Spirit—which is what you now know yourself to Be, always and everywhere, forevermore.

∞

SUMMARY POINTS

- We can rest; we have seen the Truth, which means effortless freedom from any past material experiences and concerns.
- We let go of past beliefs and thoughts that have directed and misinterpreted our perceptions; as we do so, we experience the insight and inspiration that is always available to us, but has been blocked by our erring beliefs and thoughts.
- Because we have abolished the belief that we are human and accepted the understanding that we are Spirit in form, we are prepared to accept the glories of Ascension.

- With awareness of oneness and indivisibility, we are gently lifted from a mortal, limited state of thinking to a free, immortal state of understanding—direct knowledge without the need to reason things out.

- Our eyes now see and our ears now hear the wonderful things and glorious vision that have always been prepared for us; the end of separation, division, opposition, ignorance becomes apparent; we see the heavenly new earth,

- As we apprehend and experience the One that Is, then words like "evil" and "unhappy" and "disease" and "distress" are simply dropped from our vocabulary.

- There is no longer any idea of separation, and, as experience always corresponds to our state of consciousness, recognizing ourselves as Spirit, God-being, we cannot be sick and we cannot die.

- As limitless beings we can never be satisfied with anything less than the eternal, the infinite; though we think we seek companion ship, abundant supply, freedom, what we are actually called to is the Unchangeable, Eternal Infinity.

- The One is our Life and our Heart; it is who we Are and always shall be, so we discover that we are here for a greater destiny than to function in time and space.

- As you accept the Truth of the joys and glories of your real being, your true Understanding rolls away the stone of materialism and opens the way to the supernal delights that are your inherent nature.

- You can achieve *all* good, *all* joy, *all* happiness, here, now, on Earth.

TO PONDER:

1. Consider what Heaven might look like, feel like, sound like... and then apply that to Earth: what would a heavenly Earth be like? What is the "new heaven and new earth" as you envision it?

2. What does it mean to be limitless? Unbounded? If you are indeed limitless, your awareness can be anywhere in space and time, and beyond. As energy is everywhere at once, so is your Spirit-Self; brought to this moment only by your conscious thought. Allow your awareness to expand beyond this body, this room, this region... allow it to expand across the continent and ocean – around the world. Feel, see, and hear what this beautiful planet is as you embrace it in your loving Self.

3. If everything you experience is a function of your state of consciousness, what would it take for your consciousness to be continually and constantly focused on the heavenly experience? On the Oneness, Unity, unbounded Freedom of being? Emma Hopkins says "I think this, I speak this, I write this, I *feel* this... I AM this;" therein lies your method.

TO PRACTICE:

- Remember a situation that you heard about in the news, or experienced recently and look at it from the point of view of Spirit, not making distinctions or choices, not evaluating, simply loving everyone and feeling and seeing love in everything and every action.

- Describe this new view of the situation in writing.

- Now go out in the world with the same mindset: as Spirit, we no longer choose, no longer distinguish, no longer evaluate based on certain sets of beliefs.

- Afterward, at home or in the car, describe the experience in writing, and claim it for yourself. This is who you are and how you relate to the world, as love, seeing love, being love, receiving love and becoming more fully, every day, your true Self: the Infinite Being we call God.

PART TWO:
EVIDENCE FOR
DEWATERS' SCIENCE

ACCUMULATING EVIDENCE

Lillian DeWaters was writing in the early years of the 20th century, when materialist science was just becoming the central moving force in Western culture and, paradoxically, quantum mechanics was just being discovered. Electricity was just being harnessed for household and industrial use and radio was just being invented. Psychology was not yet a discipline, and psychiatry was not a practice. In her world, the only theology was Protestant Christianity, and the only way to change from a consciousness of worry and concern to one of well-being and joy was through prayer.

Throughout the 20th century, the materialist point of view that had been developed in the European Enlightenment of the 1600s was the only accepted way to understand how the universe — and human bodies — work. Materialists believe that the only way to affect anything outside one's own body is through touch and material action. But DeWaters had grown up in Christian Science, and she and other people around her kept having experiences that contradicted that belief. More, the new science of quantum mechanics kept proving that such a mindset (or "paradigm" as Thomas Kuhn called it)[48] is inadequate to explain what actually happens.

As the century was coming to a close, therefore, a large number of experiments were conducted and theories developed that support DeWater's teachings. What follows is a brief survey of some of them.

---

[48] In his ground-breaking classic *The Structure of Scientific Revolutions.*

"SPONTANEOUS" HEALING

There are thousands of anecdotes — stories of individuals — describing cases of severe illness whose symptoms have disappeared without medical treatment. Dr. Deepak Chopra, a western-trained endocrinologist, tells many such tales in his books exploring the true nature of healing and health. In *Quantum Healing*, he describes his first such experience with an aged, dying man who, when the young doctor Chopra blithely told him he'd see him when he returned, held on to life for several weeks until his doctor came and saw him again — and died almost immediately after. Chopra also tells the reverse kind of story, as of the man who had lived comfortably with a tumor in his lungs for six years — until he was told it was cancer, at which point he became very upset and died within three months.

Chopra explains these stories with the comment that our cells "are always willing to cooperate with the mind's instructions." He tells us that "The whole body is a 'thinking body,' the creation and expression of intelligence."

MOLECULES OF EMOTION

Chopra's explanation derives from the work of Candace Pert, the researcher from the National Institute of Health who discovered what she called "molecules of emotion" in her book with the same title. The technical term for these is neuropeptides, and they are the chemicals in the body that tell the cells what to do in response to the environment. They appear everywhere in the body, in trillions of cells, almost simultaneously with whatever stimulus is affecting the emotions. Each emotion has a different set of neuropeptides associated with it, and each set of neuropeptides provides a particular set of instructions to the cells. Even a memory of an event can call forth these chemicals into every part of the body, causing all of our cells to react as if the event were occurring here and now, as is beautifully illustrated in the film "What the Bleep do We Know?"

Bruce Lipton, a molecular biologist and former professor of medicine at Stanford University, says that the chemicals that circulate throughout the body tell the cells what to do because the "brain" of the cell is the millions of receptors (which are a bit like antennae) that cover the cell's wall. When a receptor connects with a neuropeptide, it changes the chemistry inside the cell so the cell behaves differently. Recent research suggests that some of these changes may even lead to changes in the DNA, so that the cell replicates differently as well – leading to a whole new field: epigenetics, which he introduces in his book *The Biology of Belief.*

Interestingly, the cell's receptors not only respond to the chemical pattern of the molecule, they're actually responding to the electrical pattern of that chemical. This is how pharmaceutical medications work: if a drug mimics the electrical pattern of the molecule, the cell acts as if the molecule were present. It also means that, not only does the cell change its behavior when a particular chemical is present, but also when an electrical pattern imitates that chemical.

This response may explain why some people have health problems when they live too close to large electrical installations, and why "energy" healing methods are often effective. And it means that the "brain wave," or electromagnetic field generated by the brain when

we think or see or imagine something, may affect the
cell directly, as well as through the neuropeptides and
other chemicals released with those thoughts.

So, whether chemically or electrically, these medical researchers suggest, all of our thoughts are translated into instructions to the cells, and the cells grow,
die, move, or transform based on those instructions.

PLACEBOS

In his ground-breaking book, *Anatomy of An Illness*,
Norman Cousins, the popular editor of *Saturday Review*
magazine, set forth a theory of medicine that earned
him a place on the University of California at Los Angeles Medical School faculty — but is largely ignored by
doctors, today. Cousins had experienced a serious illness that had baffled his doctors, but which he was
able to overcome through a series of actions that made
sense to him, but were not recognized as having any
significant medical value in themselves. When, upon
recovery, he described his self-treatment in an article,
more than one noted physician jeeringly ascribed his
new-found health to "the placebo effect."

It's interesting to consider this statement in light of
the fact that, in tests of a new medication, the goal is
always to find out how many more people find relief
from their symptoms from the medication than from
the "placebo." ("Placebo" means "sweet word", usually a "sugar pill" or salt water, or equally ineffective
treatment.) In fact, in most studies, the "expected" rate
of relief from the placebo is 30-40%: that is, about a
third of the people in such tests recover or have significant reduction in symptoms, simply by taking the placebo. This is even more interesting when one under-
stands the rules of such tests: the new medication must

show results that are "significantly higher" than the placebo—where a "significant difference" is typically defined as 1%, 5%, or 10%. This means that a "clinically tested" medication is one which has been demonstrated to show results only slightly higher than the placebo!

Cousins was intrigued by the possibilities and did some research of his own. As documented in his book, he came to the conclusion that, "the history of medicine is actually the history of the placebo effect." As he reviewed what he called the "grim array of potions and procedures" medical practitioners have applied to illnesses over the centuries, ranging from using leeches for "bleeding" a patient to placing hot irons on the body, from force-feeding concoctions of herbs and roots to bombarding the body with radiation. he began to see that:

> ...people were able to overcome these noxious prescriptions, along with the assorted malaises for which they had been prescribed, because their doctors had given them something far more valuable than the drugs: a robust belief that what they were getting was good for them. They had reached out to their doctors for help; they believed they were going to be helped—and they were.

HANDS-ON HEALING

Another line of experimentation began in the late 1950s, when a group at McGill University in Montreal, Canada, did a series of tests of the effects of "laying on of hands." In these tests, a self-described "healer" held containers in which mice who were surgically wounded had been placed. The results showed that those mice healed significantly faster and with fewer complications than did the control group. When the same person held containers of water that would be used on barley sprouts, the plants grew taller and stronger than those in control groups. In later experiments, the researchers had other people hold the water containers and found that the plants whose water had been held by people diagnosed with significant psychological problems actually did more poorly than those whose water containers had been held by "healthy" people.

These tests, and others described by Bernard Grad in the *International Journal of Parapsychology,* were not well known, but a book describing similar tests, called *The Secret Life of Plants,* became a best-seller in the 1960s. More recently, people have been measuring and photographing electrical responses between plants at moments of trauma.

During the 1970s, Dr. Dolores Kreiger, a nursing instructor, began to teach and encourage scientific studies of a technique she called Therapeutic Touch (also known as "TT"), which is based on a similar idea. A trained practitioner learns to place a hand on or slightly above a wound or damaged area of the body, learning to "feel" the problem there and "sending" healing "energy" to the area. Thousands of people around the world have been taught the technique, many of whom are registered nurses, rigorously trained in the rules and principles of traditional, chemical and mechanical medicine. In clinical trials and many documented cases, TT has been established as a significantly effective tool. As one nurse describes her experience on the Therapeutic Touch network website:

> I started practicing TT 15 years ago and used it for a few years before I began to sense energetically. Even now, I

don't... sense many of the things my beginning students do. So why did I keep on practicing? Because I could see that people I worked with were experiencing the relaxation response, pain relief, accelerated wound healing, mental clarity, emotional balance, and/or spiritual connection.

About the same time that Dr. Krieger was introducing Therapeutic Touch to nurses, another hands-on healing method, called *Reiki* (which means "universal life energy" in Japanese) was being introduced from Japan by way of Hawaii. Again, thousands of people have been trained in the technique, many of them licensed massage therapists, trained extensively in traditional anatomy and physiology. As with TT, *Reiki* practitioners are trained to place a hand on, or slightly above, the body and feel healing "energy" flowing into damaged areas. And again, most have experienced the kind of results described by the nurse, above.

Several randomized, double-blind studies of such "hands-on" healing techniques have been completed, with large numbers of subjects. In the best-known such study, conducted by Elizabeth Wirth in 1992, non-contact TT (that is, when the practitioner holds the hands above the body, at the edge of a perceived "field," without actually touching the skin) significantly accelerated the rate of healing for deep skin wounds.

PRAYER AS TREATMENT

In 1988, at the coronary care center of the San Francisco General Hospital, Dr. Randolph Byrd changed the way scientists talk about healing. Dr. Byrd took 393 heart surgery patients and randomly assigned them to two groups. One group, of 192 patients, were prayed for on a regular basis by outside intercessors informed only of the patient's names and clinical status. The second group, of 201 patients, did not receive prayers. The experiment was set up using the standard "double-blind" method to ensure that neither the patients nor the people who cared for them knew who was receiving prayer and who wasn't. The results were remarkable: fewer than half as many of the patients who were prayed for had post-surgery problems as did those who were not prayed for.

Since then, thousands of similar experiments have been performed with similar results. While many of them were done in a way that reviewers have found problems with, more than enough have been conducted in acceptable ways to establish beyond a doubt the efficacy of "focused positive regard" as a contributory factor to healing. In these experiments, it seems that it doesn't matter how the prayer is performed, or by whom, or whether the person praying even acknowledges a belief in God. Consistently, the results have shown that patients who have loving, hopeful, thoughts expressed for them by someone on a regular basis have recovered faster and with fewer complications than those who do not.

These results have led physician Larry Dossey to proclaim that if any other therapeutic method had been found to have similar results, physicians would be sued if they didn't use them.

PERCEIVING A NEW EARTH
How individuals experience the world around them, and why there are differences, has been a huge question in both the biological and the psychological sciences for some time. The first clues actually came from another science: anthropology.

As American and European ethnologists went into the field to study other cultures, they quickly became aware that the people they were working with literally could not see something that was too far out of their model of the world to make any sense of. Then, as they began to make sense of things like radios, cameras, recording devices, some forms of clothing or medical devices, they would see it in terms that made sense to their understanding of how things are and how they work.

The field of psychological anthropology grew out of these kinds of reports, and spread into the general field of psychology, as clinicians and theoreticians sought explanations for the differences in descriptions between individuals observing the same event – a phenomenon characterized beautifully in the Japanese film, *Rashoman*. Neurologists began to explore the phenomenon as possibly related to differences in brain structure or chemicals and discovered a number of interesting facts about people witnessing the same experience:

- Different parts of the brain may be involved in different people;
- Different senses may be activated in different people, so that one hears things another doesn't, and so on;
- The eyes don't actually report directly to the brain what is going on in front of them, but instead send pre-made "film strips" based on past experiences that are familiar;
- The brain takes what's coming in from the senses (including the senses within the body) and selects only that which is familiar.

These are only a few of the kinds of things going on in the brain that contribute to the fact that different people literally perceive very different versions of what's going on around them.

As psychologists began to work with this information, they began to find that previous experiences significantly affect current perceptions, and that it was possible to change current perceptions by reducing the emotional charge on previous experiences, which is the essence of the "talking cure", "scream therapy", holotropic breathwork, "tapping", "reparenting", and many other therapeutic methods, including hypnosis.

The work of Joe Dispenza and others in helping people to shift their brain's normal neural pathways so they can, as Dispenza says, "break the habit of being themselves"[49] also helps them perceive their environment in different ways.

Social psychologists and clinicians have observed that people with a positive mindset—that is, whose brains tend to focus on what is present rather than what is lacking—tend to be healthier and have better living conditions. So, when we look across the fields of research, we can see that it's possible for someone to live in a community and have a much happier or much more distressing experience, based on their perceptual framework.

---

[49] Dispenza's book by that title outlines his process and offers numerous examples of peoples' experiences as they let go of old beliefs about who they are and what they can do and replace them with new ones.

THEORIES & MODELS

The world around us seems to be becoming more and more complex, so many scientists don't accept the traditional assumption that everything is subject to entropy and the universe would ultimately become a homeostatic field of dust. Flemish chemist Ilya Prigogine was one of them. According to Prigogine, physical structures and systems might still break down, but the process can be slowed — even reversed — in certain situations. If, he suggested, energy were constantly flowing through a structure, that structure might not decay. He called this state of being, "far from equilibrium." In such a state, he said, "dissipative structures" form that are sustained by the energy available in their environment. These ideas and the studies that supported them were so significant that they earned him a Nobel Prize.

A simple example of a dissipative structure is the funnel shape at the drain of a bathtub, formed and maintained by the flow of water through it. More complex examples include plants, animals, and our own bodies, which are maintained by the energy in the nutrients, fluids, and light we take in. Even more complex dissipative structures are communities and schools and factories. As long as energy flows through them, they maintain themselves.

With Prigogine's model, it's almost as if the universe were a flowing "stream" of energy, in which small turbulences slow down enough to become matter, which grow to become stars, which collect to become galaxies and solar systems, which create environments that become life forms, which become ecosystems and biospheres, and become self-aware beings. And, like the funnel in the bathtub, each of these structures may increase in complexity or decay into nothing, depending on the shifts in energy flows through them and through their form.

Prigogine went further and showed us that all living organisms and systems maintain or increase their own order by creating disorder in the environment around them. The embryo, developing into a baby, increases its own internal order and complexity by increasing the *dis*order inside the womb and its mother's body. Cities increase and maintain their internal order by increasing the disorder around them — in the form of garbage dumps, sewage disposal, eradication of forests, etc.. So every structure depends on its environment for the energy that sustains it, while it changes its environment by taking energy/matter in one form from it and releasing energy/matter in another form into it. In the appropriate environment, therefore, most dissipative structures will increase in order — until they change the environment too much to sustain them.

UNPREDICTABILITY

This tendency toward order or disorder in dissipative structures is, like the behavior of the subatomic particles that make up all matter, almost completely unpredictable. Depending on how complex the structure is, a very small change can have huge effects. (The "butterfly effect" is the classic metaphor illustrating this point: it suggests that the movement of a butterfly's wing in the tropics could, potentially, lead to a hurricane in the North Atlantic.) Adding a catalyst to some chemicals, a slight increase or decrease of available sunlight in a plant community (or weed patch!), a branch falling into a stream, the addition of a word or image to an idea — all may lead to the formation of whole new structures, or to the breakdown of the existing structure into chaotic heaps. And, with analytical methods, we can't know in advance which it will be.

POTENTIAL

In such structures determinism no longer holds and the law of cause and effect no longer applies. Instead, we now have a picture of the universe — and ourselves — in which a particular event need not necessarily lead to any particular outcome. In this universe we only have probabilities of an event. A diagnosis of "cancer," for example, or a forecast of "economic collapse," rather than being a prediction with a clearly determined outcome, may instead act as a "critical fluctuation," leading the system — our culture, our life — to restructure into a new form.

Another area of research that has shifted scientists from expecting deterministic outcomes to calculating possibilities and potentials is subatomic, or quantum, physics. The first thing to go was the belief that matter is solid, and that its behavior and location can be determined. As measuring tools increased in accuracy, it was found that, far from being solid, most of these hard surfaces that we see and feel and sit and stand on are, in fact, over 90% empty space!

How can this be?

Consider, for a moment, the size of our Sun and solar system. The Earth is about 8,000 miles across and 25,000 miles around. It would take about 13 *million* Earths to fill the Sun, which is about 93 million miles away. Venus is slightly smaller than Earth and about 63 million miles from the Sun. Mars is even smaller, and about 105 million miles from the Sun. And tiny

Pluto (a little larger than our Moon) is usually about 100 times further out. The next nearest star is four light-years away: that is, 60 seconds x 60 minutes x 24 hours x 365 days x 186,000 miles. That's a lot of space! (And we're in a relatively crowded section of the galaxy!)

Now, consider the structure of an atom. The electrons of an atom are proportionately as far from the nucleus as Pluto is from the Sun, and even smaller in comparative size. This means that there's far more space per unit of matter in an atom than in our solar system. And if that weren't enough, those electrons don't always act like material objects.

This was discovered in the years following World War II, in numerous experiments set up to shoot a beam of light or a stream of electrons or some other form of subatomic "stuff" toward a measuring device. Early on, a strange phenomenon was observed: these infinitesimally small objects seemed to respond to their environment! If a physicist sets up an experiment to find out how many particles, or photons, are emitted by a light source, about 80% of what is detected will be measured as particles. If the same experiment is set up so as to be able to measure the amount of waves in the light beam, about 80% of what is detected is measured as waves. More, even if the experiment is changed in the middle, the majority of subatomic "stuff" will show up as whatever the experiment is designed to measure. A new term, "wavicle," was invented to describe these things that show up as waves or particles depending on the device used to measure them.

So, scientists now look at "solid" objects as patterns of interacting waves of energy that sometimes are fields of energy and sometimes are particles bouncing off each other — and where those particles are or how they are moving can't be measured until they stop and leave a tracing on a photographic film. (Until now — a new method for "trapping" a photon was discovered in 2014 that has some potential for measuring location.)

CONSCIOUSNESS

In *Quantum Self*, physicist and philosopher Dana Zohar suggests that these wavicles can be said to be *choosing* how to show up in the experiments, and that the capacity for such choice suggests that these, the smallest possible components of matter and energy, are conscious entities.

For those of us who were taught that consciousness requires a brain, this idea is hard to accept. How can a subatomic "wavicle," so small that it can't even be measured directly, but can only be "seen" by tracing its behavior, be conscious?

If we look at a much larger structure, a single cell amoeba, we find that though it lacks eyes, it still perceives light and dark and threatening shapes and substances. And thought it lacks a brain, it still gathers food, moves in the direction of food and away from danger, and reproduces when it has begun to fail or when the environment is particularly supportive of new life.

We can look at large-scale systems like nations and see that they seem to act purposefully, as well. They, too, take in matter, energy, and information to maintain themselves, and they do it, seemingly, apart from any decisions made by any individual who might be said to "control" them. And the work of planetary researchers like James Lovelock and Lynn Margulis tells us that the biosphere as a whole seems to function that way.

Consciousness as choice-making, Zohar tells us, has been observed throughout all structures of matter and energy—from the smallest and simplest to the largest and most complex. All forms of matter and energy appear to have some rudimentary form of consciousness. (This may explain why some people experience their cars and lawn mowers as "having a mind of their own!") She calls this phenomenon, "panentheism."

Others studying this field call this idea of an ever-present, universal consciousness "panpsychism." David Chalmers,[50] and David Ray Griffin,[51] suggest that living systems, with their complex structures, seem to have significantly more, and more complex, consciousness than nonliving objects. Human consciousness, with brains and bodies that comprise the most complex systems known, may be unique in our capacity for self-awareness.

Consciousness even appears to exist in a vacuum, a space where all matter and energy has been pumped out. Physicists David Bohm and Freeman Dyson have supported the idea as inherent in particle physics. As illustrated in the film describing the Cambridge physicist Stephen Hawking's "A Brief History of Time," new wavicles "pop" into the empty space at seemingly random intervals, often to "pop" out just as quickly, but sometimes to form more stable structures. This has led some particle physicists, like Amit Goswami, to suggest that the universe *is* a field of consciousness in

---

[50] In *The Conscious Mind.*
[51] In *Unsnarling the World-Knot*

which matter and energy take form. In Deepak Chopra's terms, it's a "field of infinite possibility" present in and through all space and time.

Our reality, these scientists suggest, is a pattern of possibilities emerging from a field of consciousness, in which everything is choosing and purposeful, everywhere and always. So what has appeared random and chaotic is, in fact, carefully selected and orderly.

ARCHETYPES AND FIELDS

Human beings generally recreate what is familiar. As a result, certain behavior patterns have been recreated over and over again, through time and across cultures. These consistent patterns are called "archetypes."

Trying to understand repeated behaviors in businesses, Peter Senge and his colleagues identified eight common archetypes, described in *The Fifth Discipline*. They describe these archetypes as complex patterns of feedback loops in a system (organization, community) that often make the actual outcome vastly different from the intended outcome.

One of the most common behavioral archetypes that Senge and his group found is what he calls "Shifting the Burden." It's the classic addiction pattern. We feel uncomfortable; we find something that makes us feel better, and the next time we feel uncomfortable, we do that same thing—whether or not it will actually stop whatever is making us feel uncomfortable. And we continue to do this over and over again. After a while, as in any addiction, the goal of the system becomes "getting the fix" instead of maintaining the system. Ultimately, the system decays and the person—or the company—dies.

A variation on this one is the "Fixes that Fail" archetype, in which the solution used to solve a problem's symptom has unintended consequences that ultimately make the problem worse. In a company, sometimes investing more money into a failing operation takes the whole company down. In a body, taking anti-inflammatory drugs reduces the discomfort of swelling for the moment, but it also prevents the body from sending healing and cleansing fluids to the sore tissue — prolonging, and in some cases, preventing, the healing process.

What these archetypes have in common is that, in the name of survival, the people doing them are actually destroying themselves. Rather than observing the range of possibilities and choosing the one that has the greatest potential for achieving optimum well-being, they're taking a simple, direct action that, ultimately, leaves them worse off than when they started.

Why would they do such a thing?

The concept of archetype emerged from a psychotherapist's attempt to make sense out of the patterns he saw in the thousands of dreams his patients described. Back in the early 20th century, Carl Jung had been one of Sigmund Freud's students, but he took off on his own. Working with patients in institutions as well as individual clients, Jung saw the same stories repeated countless times. Then anthropologists began reporting stories and dreams from other cultures, and he saw the same patterns there, as well.

In *Man and His Symbols*, Jung identifies a few dozen themes, including the wicked stepmother, the kidnapped maiden, the hero's journey, the battle with a dragon or demon, and the sometimes-comforting-some-times-terrifying Earth mother, which can be found in virtually every human life. One woman may consistently replay the "abandoned maiden" story in her life and dreams, well into her seventies. A man may continually be "slaying the dragon" in every new project, even when he has a home and a wife and grandchildren—and a huge pension plan. The "class clown" can be found in every group of adolescent boys from Africa to Alaska.

Jung called these patterns archetypes because they were types that "arched over" individuals and cultures, and he suggested that they exist in a common "mind," or consciousness, that all human beings contribute to and are affected by. He called this mind, the "collective consciousness." His observations led him to think that all minds are divided into the "conscious," that which we are aware of, and the "unconscious," which we're not aware of (as Freud had suggested). He went further to suggest that this division applies to the collective mind of humanity. He developed a model of consciousness made up of three aspects: a collective and individual "super-conscious" (related to ideals and abstractions) of which we're usually not aware, each individual's personal awareness, and an individual and collective "sub-conscious," related to the body and physical world, of which we're not usually aware.

During the 1970s, a new discipline known as transpersonal psychology grew out of these ideas. Transpersonal psychologists work on the assumption that our minds are part of a larger consciousness and affect each other in far more ways than we can see in our physical behaviors. They encourage meditation,

visualization, and hypnosis as ways to clarify someone's patterns of interaction with others, and to discover what is being drawn from, or contributing to, the
collective consciousness. Transpersonal psychologists
like Angeles Arrien, Jean Houston, Joanna Macy,
Frances Vaughn, and Roger Walsh often work with
shamans and other "psychic" healers as part of their
exploration of this shared experience.

Therapists working with these ideas find that behavior patterns are often strongly affected by the
thoughts and images that people hold in their minds.
Often, as Carolyn Myss suggests in *Sacred Contracts,* we
may find that an agreement held in the collective consciousness of a couple, family, or community, locks its
members into a particular pattern of behaviors.

Transpersonal psychologists usually suggest shifting a patient's focus from the behaviors of others in the
group and concentrating on their own experience.
When patients use various tools to "stand outside" the
experience and "release attachment" to the events and
feelings associated with them, they begin to operate
from their individual super-conscious, and have access
to information and possibilities held in the collective
super-conscious.

Their results suggest that this shift in individual
consciousness can change the consciousness of everyone involved — whether or not the change is expressed
verbally to the other members of the group. Because
the collective consciousness is made up of individual
consciousness, any change in one person changes the
whole. And those people who are closely related to the
one who has changed will feel the difference most
strongly.

Biologist Rupert Sheldrake, in his *New Science of Life*, proposes the existence of a "field of "morphic resonance" (*morpho* coming from the Greek for "form" or "shape") to explain how people and other beings who are apparently far apart can be affected by each other's thoughts and actions. He suggests that whenever something occurs in nature or in our experience, it resonates with everything like it, all over the world, almost immediately.

Whenever something new happens, Sheldrake says, a new "morphogenetic" field (*genetic* coming from the Greek for "creating") is created, increasing the likelihood of similar events around the world. His classic example is that of teaching newborn rats to perform a new exercise in New York, after which rats in England learning the new exercise more quickly— though there's been no direct communication between them.

THE BIO-ENERGY FIELD

Now, as the 21st century unfolds, energy healing methods abound in the US, and around the world. They include Chinese and Japanese methods based on *Qi* (also called *chi,* and *ki)* through methods based on the Hindu idea of *prana* and the Tibetan *lung*—all of which are based on the idea that the very air we breathe is filled with subtle energies and those energies flow through the body and sustain it as directed by mind.[52] A variety of methods have been introduced by

---

[52] An over view of these methods, with an explanation of why they work, and some scripts for practicing them, may be found in the book *Calm Healing,* by Robert Bruce Newman and Ruth L. Miller.

American healers as well, perhaps the best known of which being Eric Pearls' Reconnective Healing method, explained in the film, "The Living Matrix." Many thousands of people have reported positive, lasting results using these methods, and more clinical experiments are being performed based on them each year. The U.S. National Institutes of Health has accepted these results as indicative of a human "bio-energy field," which we observe by results of action, rather than measurement.

A NEW MODEL OF MIND

By combining these various ideas, modern scientists have developed a new model of consciousness that explains many phenomena that have been unexplainable by old models. According to this model, thoughts occur not only in the individual's mind, but within the consciousness, or mind, of all humanity (Jung's collective consciousness) at the same time. This human consciousness is, then, part of the consciousness that shapes all activity on the Earth (Sheldrake's morphogenetic fields), which is part of the consciousness of the universe (Zohar's panpsyche and Goswami and Chopra's field of infinite possibilities). Any thought or action then affects the whole and all individuals within it, increasing the likelihood of a similar thought or action, and making each of us contributors to, not only our own experience, but that of the whole universe.

So, with this model and the experiments that support it, scientists of the late twentieth century confirmed and explained what our hitherto unrecognized New Thought teachers and scientists of the late nineteenth century experienced:

- thought and body are inextricably interconnected;
- thought affects all aspects of body function and experience;
- individual thought is part of a larger field of thought, a larger mind, in which all are interconnected;
- one person's thought affects not only their own body and life, but other people and their experience;
- replacing an old pattern of thought with a new one leads to new conditions in the mind, the body, and the surroundings.

And this new model explains how and why the New Thought approach transforms and heals.

DeWaters' Model in the Context of Modern Research

Lillian DeWaters was a scientist who, through study and experimentation, developed a model of mind and the universe that proved to be very effective for her students seeking ways to free themselves of physical and emotional limitations. Although expressed within the larger framework of the Christian language and tradition, her model is actually very much in line with emerging models among materialist scientists.

As more and more quantum physicists and transpersonal psychologists seek to understand the workings of the brain and the nature of consciousness, an interesting phenomenon is occurring. Rupert Sheldrake, the biologist who developed the theory of morphic resonance and has established experimentally that there is a direct connection between individuals within a species and even across some species, calls it "anatheism". Baptists will recognize the prefix "ana" as meaning again. Sheldrake is describing a movement by which generations of materialists are having to give up the idea that matter is the root of everything in favor of the idea that a consciousness penetrates and orders all that exists: a "theos" or God.

The currently (2024) acceptable term among scientists and other academics is "panpsychism," described earlier in this section as the acceptance of a self-aware intelligence that permeates all that exists and guides its development.

In DeWaters' terms, there is One beingness present throughout all that exists and nothing exists outside of that beingness.

From a systems perspective, this makes total sense. There is one whole system, which we call the universe, and within it are many subsystems, overlapping and in mutually supportive relationships within the one. Every system has a function and an order, and everything within that system contributes to the overall function and order, or it is dissolved. This means it's not possible for any individual to function in ways that do not benefit the whole for very long, and that the whole is constantly supporting the individual's development as part of the development of the whole.

In DeWaters' terms, this is the loving Presence that is guiding and supporting us through the stages of development that she calls "at-one-ment, resurrection, and ascension." The system is set up to encourage our movement through these stages in our understanding and action so that we may be more integrally part of the operation of the whole, and guide others in the process.

Transcendentalist psychologists have been working with these basic ideas since the 1970s, and have been documenting the ways in which humanity is not bound by the material limits of the body, drawing in part on the ongoing research of the Society for Psychical Research in England, which began collecting and analyzing such data in the 1800s. DeWaters undoubtedly knew about the work of the Royal Society, although she doesn't talk about it in this book.

Both groups have pretty well established that the death of the body does not mean the death of the individuality that occupied the body. Both have also established that the physical senses are not the limits of the individual's access to knowledge. More, both groups have provided ample evidence of non-material healing, to the point where energy healing methods are now included as options at the U.S. National Institutes of Health. In other words, DeWaters' experiences affecting the health of other people are increasingly common and accepted.

DeWaters goes beyond healing to suggest that it's possible to live in a world where healing is not necessary. She offers a way to perceive the world differently by shifting the brain's familiar state from one of separation and lack to one of beauty, plenty, ease, and joy. She, like all New Thought teachers, encourages entering into meditative states with the intention of experiencing things differently—with the expectation of experiencing union with the One Mind that pervades All That Is. And this is precisely what the most recent science says must be done to "rewire" the neurons' pathways and perceive the world in a new way.

The main point DeWaters makes, that the body, once it's understood as an expression of the infinite, eternal Spirit, need not die, is only recently being considered a possibility. Slowly and steadily, the barriers to immortality of the body are being broken down by a few theoretical physicists and geneticists.

For physicists, accepting that thought is energy and information, neither of which can be destroyed, is the beginning. Accepting that a mind is a field of energy governing the body, and that an individual mind is part of the larger field (the quantum field, or "panpsyche") that exists throughout the universe, means that mind never dies. It is infinite in time and space, just as the universe is. This that our experience of self cannot die.

For geneticists, the appearance of what's called "telomeres" at the end of chromosomes seemed to put a limit on the number of times cells could replicate, which meant a limit on the lifespan of the body. But recent research has established that certain mind-body practices can actually increase the number of telomeres, which, clearly, prolongs the lifetime of the body. And it happens that those practices are ones in which the individual comes to a felt experience of being at-one-with the Oneness of All That Is.

So modern science is coming around to the understanding that DeWaters expressed so clearly in this book, nearly a hundred years ago. Who We Are can live a heavenly existence, always and everywhere; our Self never dies. What we seem to be, the body, doesn't have to live only "4 score and 10" as the old adage puts it, but may live far longer. The body may even reach a state of physical Ascension. It may transform into a light-filled Spirit being—as Jesus the Nazarene, Enoch and Elijah, many Egyptian pharaohs, Buddhist lamas, and others have been reported to experience in ages past

She called her understandings a science, the Science of Ascension. Her method was indeed scientific in its approach. She observed phenomena that didn't fit current scientific thinking and explored several possible explanations, both through reasoning and experiment. She demonstrated one possibility as most effective in explaining the observed phenomena and continued to experiment with it. Today, other scientists, from very different disciplines, have verified many of her conclusions. Now we get to watch as more of them find more ways to understand how and why an individual can become totally free of the distresses of civilized life, "ascending" to new heights of being, in which no illness or poverty, no accident or disaster can affect them. Then a new paradigm will be accepted and established — a science of Spirit, rather than of Matter — and a whole new era of human potential will begin.

ABOUT THE AUTHORS

LILLIAN DEWATERS

Born in 1883, Lillian DeWaters lived in Stamford, Connecticut, and in her early teens began to study metaphysics and the Bible. She says,

> It was from the Bible that I learned to turn from all else to God direct.... What stood out to me above all else was the fact presented, that when they turned to God they received Light and Revelation; they walked and talked with God; and they found peace and freedom.

DeWaters grew up in Christian Science and became a practitioner. She published three books while actively within the Christian Science organization, but moved on in 1924, when she had an awakening experience that led to her separation from the Christian Science doctrine.

She created her own publishing company and became a prolific writer, with over 30 books published in 15 languages.

She was also a well-known teacher who taught regularly at the Church of the Healing Christ, which met at the Waldorf Astoria hotel in New York (where Emmet Fox became minister in the 1930s), and she was sought after as a healer throughout the world. All of her books were based on what she called "direct unfoldments," and each book reveals deeper Truth that serious students of metaphysics immediately recognize and treasure.

RUTH L. MILLER

Ruth L. Miller, Ph.D. is a 20th-century "Baby Boomer" who integrates new understandings of culture and consciousness in a way that "the rest of us" can understand. Working as a futurist and organizational and community development consultant, she taught in half a dozen colleges and universities around the Pacific Northwest, based on her degrees in anthropology, environmental studies, cybernetics, and systems science.

In her second career, the Rev. Dr. Miller, D.D., serves as an ordained New Thought minister in Unity, Science of Mind, and Unitarian churches around Oregon. She is the host of a regular radio program called Noetic Moments, on the science of consciousness, and also manages several websites and a YouTube channel to provide broader access to her books, interviews, classes, and presentations.

Through her many books, Miller offers modern interpretations of the writings of early New Thought teachers, along with summary points and exercises in her Library of Hidden Knowledge series (published by Atria/Simon & Schuster) and in several books published by WiseWoman Press. She also brings a deeper understanding to ongoing cultural processes and potentials in a series of books looking to the past to enhance our future, published by Portal Center Press. Her guidelines for a deeper, more effective spiritual life reach beyond traditional notions of religion, integrating the essence of the many paths of humanity's many faith traditions.

OTHER BOOKS BY LILLIAN DEWATERS

- The One: A Study of the Absolute
- The Practice of Reality
- Who Am I
- "I Am That I Am"
- The I Am Self ('I Am That I Am' Series No. 2)
- The Great Answer
- The Voice of Revelation: or Atomic Light
- The Finished Kingdom
- The Seamless Robe
- The Word Made Flesh
- The Voice of Revelation
- Light of the Eternal
- Greater Works (with The Narrow Way and The Atomic Age)
- Journeying Onward
- How To Have Dominion
- Practical Demonstration
- Loving Your Problem
- The Narrow Way
- The Story of Baby Life
- IN HIS NAME
- The Christ Within: A Study of the Absolute
- Science of Ascension: A Study of Our Being
- Science of Ascension: A Study of The Absolute
- In His Name, A Study of The Absolute
- Lifting The Veil
- Thinking Heavenward
- God is All and Light, (Companion Volume to God Is All)

Books by Ruth L. Miller

Interpretations of Early Teachers

- *As We Think, So We Are. James Allen's Guide to Transformation*
- *Coming Into Freedom, H. Emilie Cady's Lessons in Truth for the 21st Century*
- *Identifying With The Infinite: Lillian DeWaters' Science of the Absolute for the 21st Century*
- *Natural Abundance, Ralph Waldo Emerson's Guide to Prosperity*
- *One Law: Henry Drummond Explains Nature and Love*
- *The Creative Power of Thought: Thomas Troward's Metaphysics*
- *The NEW Game of Life and How to Play It: Florence Shinn's classic for the 21st century*
- *The NEW Master Key System: Charles Haanel's classic for the 21st century*
- *The NEW Science of Getting Rich: Wallace Wattles' classic for the 21st century*
- *The Spiritual Science of Emma Curtis Hopkins*
- *Unveiling Your Hidden Power: Emma Curtis Hopkins' Metaphysics for the 21st Century*

Biographies and Histories in New Thought

- *150 Years of Healing: America's New Thought Healers & Teachers*
- *Thoughts Heal: America's New Thought Healers & Teachers* (3rd edition of *150 Years of Healing*)
- *Paths of Power* series of biographies — Emerson, Holmes, The Fillmores, Cady, Hopkins, Troward

Self Help & Spiritual Support

- *Spiritual Success: Developing Your Own Daily Practice*
- *Uncommon Prayer: Beyond Religious Formulas*
- *Unlocking the Power of The Secret: 12 Keys*
- *Experiencing the Miracle: The Essential Course In Miracles for the 21st Century*

Healing Methods & Consciousness

- *Calm Healing: Mind-Body Healing Methods* with Robert B. Newman
- *Empowered Care: Mind-Body Medicine* (2nd edition of *Calm Healing*) with Robert B. Newman

Organization Development

- *Developing 3rd Generation Learning Communities: A Heuristic Discovery Process* with Kazimierz Gozdz
- *Organizations with Spirit: from Vision thru Staffing*

Our Culture's History and Future

- *Apocalypse Now? Unveiling Rather than Destroying*
- *Earth Can Still Be Home: Creating Humanity's Future* (3rd edition of *Living A New Dream*)
- *Home: Creating Humanity's Future* (2nd edition of *Living A New Dream*)
- *Language of Life: finding solutions to today's issues in ancient languages* with Milt Markewitz
- *Madonna, Magdalene, and Beyond* (2nd edition of *Mary's Power: the divine feminine hidden in western culture*)
- *To Rebalance Earth: Indigenous Wisdom for A Harmonious Future* with Milt Markewitz

Made in United States
North Haven, CT
11 September 2024

57293523R00108